Collins · *do brilliantly!*

2005 Test**Practice**

KS3 Shakespeare
Much Ado About Nothing

Test practice at its **best**

■ **Mike Gould**

■ **Series Editor: Jayne de Courcy**

William Collins' dream of knowledge for all began with the publication of his first book in 1819.
A self-educated mill worker, he not only enriched millions of lives, but also founded a flourishing publishing house.
Today, staying true to this spirit, Collins books are packed with inspiration, innovation and practical expertise.
They place you at the centre of a world of possibility and give you exactly what you need to explore it.

Collins. Do more.

Published by Collins
An imprint of HarperCollins*Publishers*
77–85 Fulham Palace Road
Hammersmith
London
W6 8JB

Browse the complete Collins catalogue at
www.collinseducation.com

10 9 8 7 6 5 4 3 2 1

ISBN 0 00 719411 0

British Library Cataloguing in Publication Data
A Catalogue record for this publication is available from the British Library

Edited by Joanne Hunt
Illustrated by Harriet Buckley, Fliss Cary, Sarah Wimperis
Production by Katie Butler
Book design by Bob Vickers
Printed and bound by Printing Express, Hong Kong

Acknowledgements
Cambridge University Press for extracts from *Much Ado About Nothing* by William Shakespeare, edited by F H Mares,
The New Cambridge Shakespeare Series, 1997 © Cambridge University Press, reproduced with permission.

Photographs
The Author and Publishers are grateful to the following for permission to reproduce photographs:
Historical Picture Archive/CORBIS (p7 top); Bettmann/CORBIS (p7 centre); Donald Cooper/Photostage (p12); Donald
Cooper/Photostage (p13); Renaissance Films/Album/AKG (p19); Royal Shakespeare Company (p20); Donald
Cooper/Photostage (p27); Donald Cooper/Photostage (p29); Renaissance Films/Album/AKG (p41).

You might also like to visit:
www.harpercollins.co.uk
The book lover's website

Contents

Section 1 Understanding the play

Section 2 How to answer Test questions

Section 3 Practice paper

How this book will help you

Test Practice KS3 Shakespeare: Much Ado About Nothing has been designed to help you gain a high level in the Shakespeare Paper of your English National Test. Here is how:

1. It provides a **detailed commentary on *Much Ado About Nothing*** covering all the areas you need to know about: plot, characters, themes and language.

2. It prepares you for the **Shakespeare Paper** by giving you expert guidance on the **techniques and skills** you need in order to answer questions well.

3. It gives you a **complete practice paper** based on the **set scenes for 2005** as well as **level indicators** and **sample answers**.

Section 1 UNDERSTANDING THE PLAY

- **Unit 1** provides a **background** to *Much Ado*, focussing on interesting facts about the play, and an introduction to life in Shakespeare's times.

- **Unit 2** consists of a **scene–by–scene commentary** on the play. The plot analysis explains clearly *what* happens, *when* it happens – and *why*. Analysis is deepened with colour-coded references to **themes** which are examined in greater detail in **Unit 4**.

- **Unit 3** looks at **character**, analysing the behaviour and motives of each of the main characters in turn. There are quotations and evidence to back up the ideas.

- **Unit 4** looks at **key themes**, expanding on the colour-coded analysis in **Unit 2**.

- **Unit 5** examines key aspects of Shakespeare's use of **language** in *Much Ado*, looking at *what* is said, *how* it is said and the *effect* this has on the audience.

Section 2 HOW TO ANSWER TEST QUESTIONS

This section covers the **key skills and techniques** you need in order to do your best in the Shakespeare Paper. It tackles the most common problem areas for students in the Test and provides you with the techniques to answer questions well.

Each of the units in **Sections 1 and 2** have the following:

QUICK CHECK

Short questions which test your understanding.

do brilliantly!

Essential hints on how to get the **TOP LEVELS** in your Test and **examples** of answers that score a high level.

Section 2 also provides:

TIP

Simple, easy-to-remember advice.

Section 3 PRACTICE PAPER

This section gives you the chance to do **two practice questions** on your set scenes from the play. It also provides:

- detailed **level indicators** showing what Test markers are looking for when awarding marks;

- **sample answers** from students **at different levels** so you can compare your work with theirs and **practise improving your answer** in order to raise the grade.

What you need to know about the Shakespeare Paper

This book is all about preparing you to write a good answer on *Much Ado* in the Shakespeare Paper. In order to prepare effectively, you need to know what is involved and be clear about what you are working towards. **Section 3** gives you practice at answering questions, but you need to keep your mind on the Test from the start of this book.

So, here's a **summary of what you are required to do in the Test**:

- You will be given **ONE question** based on your study of *Much Ado*.
- You will need to spend **45 minutes** answering it.

The question will be based on the **following scenes for 2005**:

> **Act 1 Scene 1 (lines 119–215)**
> *'Benedick, didst thou note the daughter of Signor Leonato?'*
>   to
> *'...examine your conscience: and so I leave you.'*
>   and
>
> **Act 2 Scene 3 (lines 81 to the end of the scene)**
> *'Come hither, Leonato, what was it you told me of today,'*
>   to
> *'if I do not love her I am a Jew, I will go get her picture'*

In the actual Test, **shorter extracts** from **two of these scenes** will be included on your Shakespeare Paper.

You should **base your answers on the extracts you are given in the Test.**

Finally, some extra advice

Try to see a performance of *Much Ado* (either on stage or on film). Although you are working towards a Test, you can still enjoy the play. After all, it has a great story, memorable characters, and powerful language.

Most importantly of all, imagine the play in performance as you study it and use this book. Don't forget that Shakespeare was himself an actor and wrote his plays for performance. Remember that there is an audience if there is a performance!

If you use this book to help you gain a thorough understanding of *Much Ado* and how to answer Test questions on it, there is no doubt that you will *do brilliantly*!

on 1 Secti
Section 1
1
tion 1 Sec

Brush up your Shakespeare!

We don't know when *Much Ado About Nothing* was written or first performed, but it seems likely that Shakespeare composed it before 1600. The first known performance was in 1613 and the play was very popular even then – and it remains one of Shakespeare's most performed plays today.

But, did you know...?

The original story

- There are lots of old stories in which a lover is deceived into thinking that his fiancée is unfaithful after seeing her at a bedroom window with another man. For example, the traditional Spanish romance, *Tirante the White* (from about 1400), and later the story of Phaon and Claribel in Spenser's *The Faerie Queen* (1590) both feature similar stories.

- Shakespeare would have known about these but he seems to have based *Much Ado About Nothing* on a story called *Timbreo di Cardona* by Bandello, told by an Italian writer in 1554. In this version, Claudio is recognisable in the character of Timbreo and Hero is named Fenicia. However, one notable difference is that Timbreo's companion, Girondo (the Don John character) falls in love with Fenicia, too, and only decides to ruin the relationship when she rejects him. Girondo eventually confesses and then marries Fenicia's younger sister!

Missing mothers

- Where have all the mothers gone? In some early recorded versions of the play, Leonato has a wife called Innogen, although she never speaks. In the version we know today she is not in the play at all. Beatrice too has no mother. Perhaps this is because Shakespeare needed the female characters to be isolated, or independent.

Playing the part

- The actor **David Garrick** liked the part of Benedick so much that, from 1748 onwards, he played it every year for 30 years!

- Actor **Robert Lindsay**, who starred as grumpy dad Ben Harper in 'My family', played Benedick in the BBC production of 1984.

- Hollywood star, **Keanu Reeves**, best known for his action roles in *Speed* and *The Matrix*, played Don John in Kenneth Branagh's film of 1993.

Making improvements?

- In the late 1600s, **Sir William Davenant** adapted many of Shakespeare's plays into a 'low' form of opera which included many songs and dances. In 1662 he put *Much Ado* with another of Shakespeare's plays, *Measure for Measure*, called it *The Law Against Lovers*, and added some songs!

- In 1723 **Charles Johnson** renamed the play *Love in a Forest* adding scenes from other Shakespeare plays, such as *A Midsummer Night's Dream, As You Like It, Tweflth Night* and *Love's Labour's Lost*.

- **Kenneth Branagh's** film version (1993) opens with Beatrice and the others picnicking outside and then rushing in with excitement at the approach of Don Pedro and his men.

FACT AND FICTION?

- In 1458, an illegitimate Prince of the House of Arragon, named John, became the ruler of Sicily. Perhaps Shakespeare based the character of Don John on this man. However, in *Much Ado About Nothing*, Don John is much less successful. He is defeated by his half-brother (Don Pedro) before the play begins, tries to cause many problems for the other characters, but is captured after he tries to escape at the end of the play.

Life in Shakespeare's times

William Shakespeare

> I know that Shakespeare was alive a long time ago, but do I really need to know what life was like in his day?

To enjoy the play, you don't. But it does help if you know a little about the history. William Shakespeare's baptism was recorded in **1564** and he died in **1616**. He lived through the reigns of two English monarchs. The first was **Elizabeth 1**, who reigned from **1558–1603**. Her reign was one of **great achievements** in the arts, exploration and scientific discovery.

Adventurers, such as **Sir Walter Raleigh**, sailed to distant lands, and brought back news of the places they visited and the people who lived in them. This was really exciting for Shakespeare and his contemporaries.

However, this golden age was also a time of **civil unrest**. Shakespeare and the actors in his company would have been very aware of the political situation that faced their monarch. They would have noted the **lack of an heir** to the throne and the **continuing disputes** over **Elizabeth's 'right' to be Queen**.

There were many plots against Queen Elizabeth I, and Shakespeare would have been aware of events such as the **Essex rebellion** (when the Earl of Essex attempted a raid on the Queen and London and was later executed for treason), and the **execution of rival Mary Queen of Scots** for plotting against the Queen.

Some people think that Don John's sabotage is a reference to the Essex rebellion, but if it is it is pretty thin, as Don John does no lasting damage, and as far as we know, is not likely to be executed.

> Who was the second monarch? After all, Elizabeth I died in 1603 and Shakespeare didn't die until 1616.

The second monarch was **James 1**, who lived from **1603–1625**. It was James who granted Shakespeare's acting company a royal licence, and made them **'King's Men'**.

The arts continued to develop. Many **new theatres** were built during this period and **literature flourished**.

The original Globe Theatre, London

In Shakespeare's time **theatre was very popular** – at all levels of society. It was popular entertainment and **not just for the upper class**. Many early performances of Shakespeare's plays would have been performed in the courtyards of inns (pubs) where the audience would watch from the street and from the galleried balconies around the courtyard.

Other popular events in Shakespeare's time were **masques** (masked balls) which combined music, poetry, scenery and costumes. Masques were especially popular between 1600 and 1640 at court. The wearing of masks at a ball (as we see at the start of *Much Ado*) would have been familiar to many theatre-goers. Indeed, Shakespeare makes use of it in other plays, such as *Romeo and Juliet* where the lovers also meet masked and are unaware as they fall in love that they are from rival families.

QUICK CHECK

1. What were the names of the Claudio and Hero characters in Bandello's story?
2. Who was the female character who appeared in some early versions of *Much Ado About Nothing*?
3. How can we tell that David Garrick liked playing the part of Benedick?
4. What real life character resembled Don John?
5. What were masques?
6. What other play by Shakespeare features characters wearing masks?

Keep to the point

do brilliantly !

Although the information on these two pages is interesting, do not fall back on writing about Shakespeare, or his times, when you don't have much to say about the key scenes in the Test! **Stick to the scenes you are studying.** Outside information is only useful if it enables you to say something relevant about the character, language or themes.

2 The plot: scene by scene

Act 1: Scenes 1 to 3

There is a kind of merry war betwixt Signor Benedick and her.

Scene 1 Don Pedro's arrival

The play opens in front of Leonato, Governor of Messina's, house. A messenger comes to tell him that Don Pedro, Prince of Arragon, is passing through Messina on his return from a victorious battle. Beatrice, Leonato's niece, asks if Benedick is part of the company but hides her interest with cutting remarks about him.

Don Pedro arives with Don John (his illegitimate half-brother), Claudio and Benedick. Beatrice and Benedick trade insults, while Claudio, attracted by Hero's beauty, falls in love with her.

Claudio asks Benedick what he thinks of Hero, but Benedick says that marriage is for fools and insults Hero's appearance. Don Pedro says he will pretend to be Claudio during the masked ball that evening and will speak to Hero and her father on Claudio's behalf.

Commentary

- The **situation** is explained – Beatrice and Benedick's relationship and Don Pedro's arrival.
- The key **characters** are introduced.
- The first plan is made (Don Pedro wooing Hero for Claudio) which **starts the action** straight away.

Themes

Love and marriage: Already we see the contrast between different attitudes to marriage. Claudio says, '*In mine eye, she is the sweetest lady that ever I looked on.*' whereas Benedick appears not to want to marry: '*I will live a bachelor.*'

Tricks and deception: Don Pedro offers to pretend to be Claudio and woo Hero for him.

Self-deception: Benedick and Beatrice swear that they hate the opposite sex – and each other, but already **the audience** suspects they are disguising or hiding their true feelings.

Scene 2 Antonio gets it wrong

Antonio reports to his brother Leonato that he has overheard Don Pedro telling Claudio that he is in love with Hero. Leonato says that he will wait to hear this from Don Pedro, but will tell his daughter about the Prince's intentions.

Themes

Tricks and deception: The idea of someone being **overheard** or secretly observed is central to the play, as are the confusions that arise from it.

Commentary

- On the face of it, this is an unimportant scene, but it might be used to **suggest the passing of time** and the preparation for the masked ball (hence the reference to '*this music*').
- The mistake made by Antonio has no real effect, except that it does hint at what is to come – more **mistaken identity**.

> Come, come, let us thither, this may prove food to my displeasure.

Scene 3 Don John is introduced

Don John speaks with Conrade, one of his followers, explaining his behaviour ('*I cannot hide what I am: I must be sad when I have cause…*'). Conrade advises Don John to act civilly to his brother (Don Pedro).

Borachio, another of Don John's men, arrives and tells Don John that he has overheard news of the intended marriage of Claudio and Hero. Don John wonders if he can make mischief for Claudio, whom he dislikes for being in his brother's favour.

Themes

Tricks and deception: Borachio **hides** '*behind the arras*' (a curtain) and **overhears** the Prince's plans, much as Antonio's servant did earlier in Scene 2 (although Borachio – unlike Antonio – hears correctly).

Status and honour: Don John's villainy is partly due to his feeling that he has been wronged and has no power (being a half-brother only): '*…that young start-up hath all the glory of my overthrow*'.

Commentary

- The **darker side**, which later on will come to dominate this comedy, is introduced here – Don John's **jealousy** and **bad humour**.

- The **seeds are sown** for what will happen later as Don John says: '*…if I can cross him (Claudio) any way, I bless myself…*'

QUICK CHECK

1. In (and around) whose house does the action take place?
2. Who is due to arrive at the start of the play?
3. Who does Beatrice ask about?
4. Who does Claudio fall in love with?
5. What is Benedick's view of marriage?
6. Who is Don John?
7. How does Borachio hear the news of Claudio's love for Hero?
8. Why does Don John plan to make trouble for Claudio?

Less can mean more

do brilliantly!

High-attaining students often look beyond what is obvious. Take Hero and Claudio. On the surface, this is a romantic match – they fall in love. Yet where is the evidence of 'love'?

But think about **what *does not* happen**. Unlike Benedick and Beatrice they have exchanged words, good or bad. Have they even properly met before? Benedick and Beatrice have 'history' between them – they know what they are getting!

Act 2: Scenes 1 to 3

Scene 1 Masks and mischief

Leonato, Hero and Beatrice talk before the dancing begins. Beatrice complains that there is no man who can match her spirit, but Hero obediently agrees to her father's request to accept the Prince. Everyone puts on masks for the ball, Don Pedro talks to Hero privately while Benedick and Beatrice insult each other.

Don John makes Claudio jealous by saying that Don Pedro plans to wed Hero himself. Claudio thinks he has lost Hero. However, when Don Pedro tells Claudio that Hero has agreed to marry him, Claudio's jealousy turns to joy.

Now that marriage between Claudio and Hero is arranged, Don Pedro decides to bring Beatrice and Benedick together through a series of deceptions, aided by all present.

Themes

Tricks and deception: Everyone wears masks; Antonio tries (and fails) to fool Ursula (Hero's maid); Beatrice speaks to Benedick as if he is someone else (and insults him); Don John pretends to think Claudio is Benedick so he can 'reveal' that Don Pedro really loves Hero. The scene ends with Don Pedro and all present planning the next deception (of Beatrice and Benedick).

Love and marriage: This scene follows the process of Claudio pursuing Hero (through Don Pedro's courtship). It sees the development of Benedick's relationship with Beatrice, whose description of love and marriage as a 'Scotch jig', hints at the romantic twists to come before the play's resolution.

Commentary

- This scene **sets the tone** for the play – it is full of misunderstandings, jokes, and a battle of the sexes. As Beatrice says, '…*wooing, wedding, and repenting, is as a Scotch jig.*' Masks are put on, people come and go, and the audience hears one quick conversation, then another, and as soon as one plan is finished another is hatched. It is fast paced and lively – like a Scottish jig (dance).

- We witness the **'spark'** between Benedick and Beatrice through their exchange of insults, and Claudio's acceptance of his 'loss': '*farewell therefore, Hero!*'.

- Hero's obedience and Beatrice's 'spirit' are **contrasted**, as are Claudio and Benedick's approaches.

Scene 2   Don John and Borachio's plot

Borachio suggests a plot to ruin Claudio's marriage plans. He will arrange to meet with Margaret, Hero's gentlewoman, at Hero's window in the middle of the night. This will fool Don Pedro and Claudio into believing that Hero is having an affair. Don John agrees to pay a thousand ducats to Borachio for doing this.

Commentary

● This short scene **provides a parallel** to what has just happened in Scene 1. Whereas Don Pedro's plans are to create **joy** – and **love** (between Beatrice and Benedick), Don John and Borachio's plans are to create **sorrow** and **mischief**.

Themes

Status and honour: Borachio conceives a scheme in return for money – and money means status. (He later boasts of his idea to Conrade, showing that he is 'proud' of what he has done – amongst villains, it gives him status.)

Tricks and deception: Most of the scene is taken up with the mechanics of the deception – how it will be done, and Borachio seems to take pleasure in his cleverness.

…she should so dote so on Signor Benedick, whom she hath in all outward behaviours seemed ever to abhor.

Is't possible? Sits the wind in that corner?

Scene 3   Benedick is fooled

Benedick is in the orchard considering Claudio's sudden change from soldier to soppy lover when Don Pedro, Claudio, and Leonato approach. Benedick hides, but does not realise they have seen him. They then announce that Beatrice loves him but that they are worried that Benedick will mock her if he finds out.

Benedick is completely fooled. By the end of the scene, he is weighing up the benefits of marriage and reflecting on his past behaviour. Beatrice arrives to call him in to dinner. He now believes her sharp comments are actually declarations of love.

Themes

Love and marriage: A mock sentimental idea of love is presented here. We are told Beatrice '…*falls, weeps, sobs, beats her / heart, tears her hair, prays, curses…*' which we know to be far from the truth about the strong-willed, witty Beatrice. However, it works on Benedick who believes what he hears.

Tricks and deception: The whole scene is a plot to trap Benedick – at one point Claudio even says, '*Bait the hook well, this fish will bite.*' Benedick certainly does!

Self-deception: Benedick's long speech at the start of the scene shows how highly he thinks of himself – but is he saying all this to convince himself? Perhaps he feels secretly envious of the younger Claudio who has found love?

Commentary

● This scene marks the start of **Benedick's real transformation**; it is here that his love for Beatrice first shows itself.

● Don Pedro, Leonato, and Claudio's plot is especially clever because they too pretend to be amazed by Beatrice's love for Benedick. As Don Pedro says (to Claudio). '*You amaze me, I would have / thought her spirit had been invincible against all assaults of / affection.*'

QUICK CHECK

1. What item of clothing leads to the tricks and confusion in Scene 1?

2. How does Don John make Claudio jealous in Scene 1?

3. Scene 1 ends with Don Pedro suggesting that it would be good to trick two people into falling in love. Which two?

4. In Scene 2, what does Borachio suggest in order to ruin Claudio and Hero's marriage plans?

5. How do Claudio, Leonato and Don Pedro trick Benedick?

6. In Scene 3, Benedick begins the scene by criticising Claudio for acting like a soppy, married man. How has Benedick changed by the end of the scene?

7. What is Benedick's reaction to Beatrice's sharp comments when she appears in Scene 3?

Write in an imaginative way

do brilliantly!

Examiners mark hundreds of scripts. Why should yours stand out? The answer is, by the quality of your writing. Shakespeare uses **metaphors** – why shouldn't you?

For example, when talking about Don John's plotting you could say:

'Bitter seeds are sown for what will happen later...'

or

'Despite the general playfulness of this act, a dark cloud has appeared on the horizon, and it will grow larger as the play progresses...'

...be cunning in the working this, and thy fee is a thousand ducats.

Act 3: Scenes 1 to 5

Scene 1   Beatrice is fooled!

...nature never framed a woman's heart Of prouder stuff than that of Beatrice...

Hero arranges for Beatrice to overhear a conversation about Benedick's love-sickness and his desire for Beatrice. Beatrice listens while Hero and her waiting lady, Ursula, discuss how Beatrice would only make fun of Benedick if she knew. Beatrice is fooled and vows to love Benedick if he will have her.

Themes

Love and marriage: We are told a lot about the way Beatrice treats men, '*So turns she every man the wrong side out, / And never gives to truth and virtue...*' But remember that it is Hero who says this, a younger, more naive woman, who has yet to face disappointment in the world.

Tricks and deception: We see parallels in the deceptions of Beatrice and Benedick. Both Claudio and Hero talk of the deception in terms of 'bait'. Hero says: '*...that her ear lose nothing / Of the false sweet bait that we lay for it.*' (Claudio spoke similarly about Benedick in Act 2 Scene 3).

Self-deception: Unlike Benedick, who has a long speech at the beginning of the previous scene, Beatrice is silent until just before the end. Her words, when they come, display a very different Beatrice, shocked that she has misunderstood for so long the effect she has had: '*What fire is in mine ears? Can this be true?*'

Commentary

● This scene is, of course, the twin to Act 2 Scene 3 in which Benedick is fooled by Don Pedro and company. Similar techniques are used here: the plotters speak, while the person to be tricked hides, believing themselves unnoticed.

● However, in the previous scene, Don Pedro's group flattered Benedick as one way of fooling him, calling him a '*proper man*', '*very wise*' and '*valiant*'. Here, Hero and Ursula criticise Beatrice in order to fool her, Hero says: '*she cannot love, / Nor take no shape nor project of affection, / She is so self-endeared.*'

● In both scenes the person being fooled hears wonderful things about their 'admirer'. In this scene, Benedick is described as '*so rare a gentleman*' and with an '*excellent good name*'.

● Both Beatrice and Benedick hear that the other's love is a secret due to the fact that he/she will scorn or mock the other. Hero says: '*Disdain and scorn ride sparkling in her eyes...*'

Scene 2   Don John makes his move

Don Pedro, Claudio, and Leonato make fun of Benedick saying he looks pale and depressed – as well as clean and newly-shaven. They tell him he must be in love. Benedick refuses to listen and leaves to speak privately with Leonato.

Don John joins Don Pedro and Claudio and accuses Hero of being unfaithful. He says he wants to save Claudio from a shameful marriage, and he will prove her disloyalty. Don John says he will take them that night to Hero's bedroom window where they will see her with another lover, the very night before her wedding. Claudio swears that if it turns out to be true, he will shame Hero at their wedding in front of the whole congregation.

Commentary

- This scene switches from the **light-hearted comedy** surrounding Benedick's lovesick behaviour, to the **nasty and vindictive trickery** of Don John. As Don Pedro says at the end: '*O day untowardly turned!*' (What a turn for the worse!).

- Although the **audience** knows Hero is innocent, Claudio and Don Pedro do not – and the idea of shaming her in front of everyone is an unpleasant idea in itself. It is also interesting how they do not question or mistrust Don John and how little they trust Hero.

Themes

Tricks and deception: The key deception of the plot is put in place here, but it can only work because both Claudio and Don Pedro are so gullible. That Claudio even listens to the accusation shows how little he knows of Hero – this makes him easy to trick.

Self-deception: If Claudio knows so little of Hero, what is his love based on? He has deceived himself that romantic looks, and traditional courtship are enough.

Love and marriage: The deception therefore highlights a weakness in the relationship between Claudio and Hero. Claudio claims to love Hero desperately and yet he fell in love with her from sight only and does not know her very well. This contrasts with Beatrice and Benedick's relationship.

Status and honour: Both Claudio and Don Pedro's thoughts, on hearing of Hero's behaviour, turn immediately to how they will '*shame her*' at the wedding. This is, presumably, to uphold their own status and honour by punishing her for making them look stupid.

Disloyal?

The word is too good to paint out her wickedness…

Scene 3   Treachery is revealed

The Watch (local police) assemble and receive muddled instructions from Dogberry and Verges to be alert for enemies of the Prince. They overhear Borachio boast to Conrade about how he has just earned a thousand ducats from Don John. Borachio explains that he did this by fooling Claudio and Don Pedro into believing that Hero met him at her window. In fact he had met Hero's maid Margaret. The watchmen step forward and arrest Borachio and Conrade for this treachery.

Themes

Tricks and deception: The idea of people overhearing others and using that information is again present, though this time for honourable purposes.

Status and honour: Dogberry has a clear sense of his own importance and status; the humour comes from his pompous attempts to appear educated, and failing miserably.

Commentary

● This scene – almost halfway through the play – introduces the new characters of Dogberry, Verges and the Watch – all **comic** characters, but presented as **decent** and **honest**.

● Their **lack of intelligence** (for example, mixing up words by mistake: Dogberry calls one of the Watch officers 'senseless' when he means 'sensible') contrasts with the elaborate wit of Don Pedro, Benedick and others.

● The scene is also important because it **lets the audience know** that Don John's treachery might be revealed – at some point.

Scene 4   Hero prepares for her wedding

Hero is in her room preparing for her wedding. She is frantically trying things on, nervously getting ready, with maidservants coming in and out of the room. Beatrice arrives, but seems distracted – saying she is '*exceeding ill*' and '*sick*'. Margaret teases Beatrice, saying she might be in love, just like Benedick.

…I am exceeding ill, heigh ho!

For a hawk, a horse or a husband?

Themes

Love and marriage: This scene portrays the intimate moments of the bride preparing. We see that Hero's heart, however, is heavy. Beatrice too is 'sick' from love and this gives Margaret the opportunity to wittily expose Beatrice's feelings.

Commentary

● This short scene – a **busy, active interlude** before the grander drama of what is to come – is typical of Shakespeare.

● Another focus of the scene is to stress how much **Beatrice has changed** – she is now the fool who is in love (and doesn't seem to know it) and is even outwitted (in jokes) by Margaret, her cousin's maid.

● Hero says her '*heart is exceeding heavy*' – does she sense that **not everything will go to plan**?

Scene 5   Dogberry has news for a busy Leonato

The Constable, Dogberry, meets with Leonato to tell him the Watch has taken two prisoners during the night, and they need to be questioned. Unfortunately, Leonato is in a hurry to leave for the church with his daughter, Hero, and cannot make sense of Dogberry and Verges' confusing explanation. (They claim to have 'comprehended' two villains, when of course they mean 'apprehended'). Leonato orders them to carry out the interrogation themselves.

I would fain know what you have to say

Commentary

- This scene creates **comedy** as we are encouraged to laugh at Dogberry, Verges and the Watch because of the way that they mix up their words, and their simple behaviour.

- However, perhaps there is more to it than that. Their confused language creates **dramatic tension**. The first scene in which they appear (Scene 3) might make the audience wonder if such people can really keep Borachio and Conrade safely in custody.

- This scene is frustrating because we want Dogberry and Verges to be clear and precise about what has been done, but Leonato loses patience and leaves. This frustration **creates tension** in the audience, who are willing the truth to come out.

Themes

Status and honour: We see here the clash between the private (the family wedding) and the public/civil (the criminal interrogation). The truth is, Leonato, the Governor, has little time for Dogberry, the Constable. If he knew that his daughter's happiness depended on him he might see things differently.

QUICK CHECK

1. In Scene 1, whose idea is it to 'set up' Beatrice to fall in love with Benedick?
2. Scene 1 can be twinned with an earlier one – which?
3. How does Benedick look and behave when he appears in Scene 2?
4. What does Claudio vow to do if it turns out that Hero has been seen with another man?
5. Who gives confusing instructions to the Watch in Scene 3?
6. Which two characters are overheard discussing Don John's plan to shame Hero?
7. In Scene 4, how does Beatrice behave when she enters?
8. What is Margaret's explanation for Beatrice's behaviour?
9. What problem is there with Dogberry and Verges' explanations to Leonato in Scene 5?
10. Why is Leonato in a hurry?

How a scene achieves its effects

 do brilliantly!

In the Test, it is vital that you write about the effect of a scene on the audience. Take Dogberry, Verges and the Watch. Their confused language is amusing, but equally importantly, it creates **dramatic tension** as we see in Scene 5. However a different sort of tension would be felt in Scene 4 when we (the audience) know that Hero's wedding preparations are all in vain. When the audience knows what the characters do not this is known as **dramatic irony**.

Act 4: Scenes 1 and 2

Scene 1 Claudio and Hero's ruined wedding

Everyone meets at the church for the wedding of Hero and Claudio. When the Friar asks Claudio if he is there to marry Hero, he says no. Claudio then tells Leonato to take his daughter back, because she has betrayed him with another man. Claudio says he has proof she is unfaithful, and Don Pedro and Don John back up his accusations.

Hero faints, and Don John, Don Pedro and Claudio leave. For a moment there is a thought she may be dead. Leonato feels that this is the best thing, due to the shame, but she recovers. Beatrice, Benedick, and the Friar begin to suspect that Don John is behind the accusations. The Friar suggests they let people think Hero has died. Claudio will begin to feel guilty and in the meantime they will try to find out the truth. Leonato agrees to this course of action.

Left alone together Benedick confesses his love to Beatrice, who finally admits that she loves him also. To prove his love, Beatrice asks Benedick to take revenge for the wrong done to Hero. He agrees to challenge Claudio.

Commentary

- This scene is the dramatic heart of the play and, because the **audience** knows Hero to be innocent, it is all the more powerful.

- Claudio's words, that Hero is a '*rotten orange*', and those of her own father that she has '*foul-tainted flesh*', are shocking and unpleasant, and we feel for Hero. The speed with which Claudio **rushes to condemn** Hero shows that he is still young – and **lacks wisdom**.

- **In contrast**, Beatrice and the Friar both realise something is not right. Even Benedick sees that Don John may be behind it all, he says: '*The practice of it lives in John… / Whose spirits toil in frame of villainies.*'

Themes

Self–deception: Don Pedro and Claudio suffer self-deception as they believe the lies about Hero. Leonato is also guilty of this – at least initially.

Love and marriage is mixed here with **Status and honour:** Claudio is not hurt at Hero's betrayal simply because he loves her; he is hurt because his pride is wounded. He is an important young lord and she has brought '*shame*' on him. She has shown herself not to be honourable enough to be worthy of his hand. This explains his public denouncement of Hero. Leonato's despairing words are driven by the shame brought on his family. Hero's dishonour would demonstrate to Leonato that she does not respect and love her father enough to prevent this shame from falling on him. Note also the status of the Friar (the man of God), for he believes Hero's innocence and convinces Leonato to think more rationally.

Deception: Don John can stand by and admire the fruits of his deception – it has perhaps worked far better than he had hoped. This whole scene has come about because of him.

> Oh villain! Thou wilt be condemned into everlasting redemption for this.

Scene 2 Conrade and Borachio are interrogated

The Constables meet and form an 'assembly' (or 'dissembly' as Dogberry calls it!) to interrogate Borachio and Conrade. Despite Dogberry's misuse of words and phrases, the Sexton successfully accuses Borachio and Conrade of plotting against Hero, who everyone believes to be dead. We are also told that Don John has secretly fled.

Commentary

- The **deception is revealed** and the path to resolving the problems begins.
- There is **comedy** to be found in the language of Dogberry, as he **confuses his words**.
- The audience get a sense that the action is coming to a resolution as the **dramatic tension** of the previous 'constables' and wedding scenes subsides. This is the first phase cleared up – the deception is exposed. Harmony is not yet restored but we leave this scene with the impression that, somehow, it will be.

Themes

Tricks and deception: In this scene, the deception is fully out in the open. The facts have all been confirmed and Don John's disappearance earlier confirms his guilt and that of his men. We feel here that there is unlikely to be a way out for Borachio – the deception is coming to an end.

Status and honour: Dogberry continues to see himself as a man due respect and honour. When Conrade calls him a '*coxcomb*' (a fool) and an '*ass*', it wounds him deeply. He is not an intelligent or a noble man, yet it is he who has solved the crime. Without Dogberry, the mix-up would not have been resolved. So, again, the high status characters require the intelligence of the lower status ones in order to solve the confusion.

QUICK CHECK

1. Who is getting married?
2. What does Claudio tell Leonato?
3. How does Claudio describe Hero?
4. Who backs up Claudio's accusations against Hero?
5. What is Hero's reaction when she is accused?
6. Who are convinced Hero isn't guilty?
7. What does the Friar suggest they should do?
8. Who are interrogated by Dogberry and the others in Scene 2?
9. Why does it take some time for the accusation to be made?
10. What do we find out about Don John?

Key scenes

do brilliantly!

Certain scenes appear to be at the heart of a play, for example Act 4 Scene 1 is vital to *Much Ado*. But there is a **paradox** at work here. (A paradox is when two ideas seem to contradict each other.)

Much Ado is a comedy. Yet Act 4 Scene 1 has little that is comic about it. Even the conversation between Beatrice and Benedick at the end only leads to more serious matters – Benedick agreeing to kill Claudio. So, is there any way this scene could be directed more comically? Could Hero's fainting be over–dramatic and ridiculous? Could Don John play his part like a pantomime villain with boos and hisses from the audience? Or could Claudio behave like a silly, spoilt boy?

If you want to get a higher Test level, remember that labels such as 'comedy' and 'tragedy' are very general – most drama contains elements of both.

Act 5: Scenes 1 to 4

Scene 1   Don Pedro and Claudio are challenged

An angry Leonato confronts Don Pedro and Claudio. Leonato challenges Claudio to a duel to regain the honour of his daughter. Antonio, Leonato's brother, joins in the challenge, but Claudio and Don Pedro refuse to fight. Antonio and Leonato leave, promising revenge.

Benedick then appears, and challenges Claudio to a duel for the honour of Hero. Claudio and Don Pedro make fun of him, thinking he is joking. As Benedick leaves, he tells Don Pedro that his brother, Don John, has fled Messina and that they have falsely accused and killed an innocent lady.

The constables bring Borachio who confesses his part in the deception, revealing Don John's villainy. Don Pedro and Claudio are shocked and devastated by the news. Claudio remembers how he first loved Hero. Leonato hears the news about Don John, but rather than blaming him or Borachio, he says Don Pedro and Claudio are the real villains – they caused the death of Hero by believing what was said about her. Don Pedro and Claudio ask Leonato to punish them in whatever way he chooses. Leonato commands them to proclaim Hero's innocence to the people of Messina and demands that Claudio write an epitaph for Hero's grave. Also, Claudio must marry an as-yet unseen niece the next day.

Commentary

- The drama in this scene comes in the fall from grace of Don Pedro and Claudio.

- The scene begins with them mocking Benedick and laughing at his challenge. Dramatic irony is very much at work in this scene; whilst Don Pedro and Claudio feel they can laugh off Leonato, Antonio and Benedick's challenges, we know their jokes are hollow.

- When the truth about Don John's villainy is revealed, Claudio says '*I have drunk poison*', meaning as he heard the truth it felt like poison was going through his body.

- By the end of the scene Claudio and Don Pedro are meek, and ready to accept any punishment.

Themes

Status and honour: Clearly, the anger that drives Leonato – and then Antonio – to challenge Claudio and Don Pedro, is to do with this theme. Leonato and his brother believe that the family honour has been wronged – as Leonato says, '*Hero is belied, / And that shall Claudio know, so shall the prince, / And all of them that thus dishonour her.*'

Self-deception: Don Pedro and Claudio continue to decieve themselves and believe the falsehood. Self-deception drains out of them as they hear Borachio's confession.

I know not how to pray your patience, Yet I must speak, choose your revenge yourself...

Scene 2 Benedick and Beatrice meet in the garden

Benedick meets Beatrice and they repeat their love for each other. Benedick tells Beatrice he has challenged Claudio. Then Ursula, Hero's gentlewoman, enters and tells them that Don John was behind everything – though he has now fled.

Commentary

- This short scene serves to emphasise the **developing relationship** between Beatrice and Benedick, they are alone here and, unassisted, declare their feelings for each other.

- The scene also allows Ursula to **sum up** for us what has recently happened – she explains that Hero was falsely accused and that Claudio and Don Pedro were tricked.

Themes

Love and marriage: Essentially, this scene is about Beatrice and Benedick's growing love: we see that there is tenderness between them as Benedick asks: '*...for which of my bad parts didst thou first fall in love with me?*' There is honesty here too, which makes Beatrice's reply all the more truthful ('*For them all together...*') We also see the honesty they share as Benedick says: '*Thou and I are too wise to woo peaceably.*'

Scene 3 Claudio comes to the church to remember Hero

Claudio and Don Pedro come with lighted candles to Leonato's family monument. Claudio recites an epitaph (a verse on someone's death) to Hero and they remain there, solemnly and respectfully, until morning.

Themes

Self-deception: Claudio is still deceived, in that he believes Hero to be dead, but the more important self-deception has been lifted. He appears changed here; gone is the youthful pride and arrogant, impulsive behaviour. He is ready for solemn prayer and reflection.

Status and honour: This scene is as much about Hero's reputation being restored as anything else, and it is interesting to note that the Prince (of highest status) and the young lord are made to do such public penance.

Done to death by slanderous tongues, was the Hero that here lies:

Commentary

- Claudio is now shown as a **humble young man,** paying respect to the young woman he harmed.

- This **sombre scene** acts as the **counterpart to the one** to come (the final scene) which will reveal the truth, and bring joy.

Scene 4 Hero is revealed – and two weddings take place

While Leonato awaits Claudio's arrival, Benedick asks the Friar to marry him and Beatrice as well. Hero and Beatrice come forward, masked. Claudio declares himself husband to the woman he stands beside, and Hero reveals herself.

Then Beatrice and Benedick argue about whether they really love one another, but their friends produce secret love poems each has written. Benedick kisses Beatrice to 'stop' her jokes and teasing, and all join together in a dance to celebrate the two marriages.

The scene ends with a messenger telling of Don John's capture, and how he has been brought back to Messina. Benedick says they should not think about him till the next day, but should dance instead.

Commentary

- This scene provides the **resolution to the action**, gathering together all the loose ends.
- Leonato's deception of Claudio is lifted, and Hero is **unmasked**.
- Benedick and Beatrice uncover the manner in which they were 'tricked' into loving each other, but this revelation is harmless, and does not lead to their separation.
- The final news about Don John tells us that the **villain has not got away with his crime**.

Themes

The key themes of the play are brought together in this scene.

Love and marriage: It is interesting to note that this marriage of Claudio's is not based on love: the 'niece' Claudio is to marry is a stranger. In the end though, both marriages are 'love marriages' and love rules the day!

Tricks and deception: There is one final trick/deception here, the masking of Hero – but it is a test to see if the new Claudio, more humble, can have faith – something he failed to have before.

Self–deception: The unmasking of Hero is also symbolic. It represents the newness of their relationship, now that Claudio has learnt his lesson. The self-deception they have both suffered is lifted; they now see each other as they really are.

Status and honour: Leonato's family honour is restored. Claudio becomes honourable, as he has done wrong, been punished, and learned from it. He is now worthy of Hero – whom he once spurned as '*...but the sign and semblance of her honour*'.

What's in a word?

*do **brilliantly**!*

To gain a higher Test level, it is important you **interrogate** words, like a detective. What does this mean? Why is this said at this point? What is the reaction to these words?

Take Benedick's last words to Beatrice, '*Peace I will stop your mouth*' (Scene 4). What should you read into this? Now that Benedick has Beatrice, does he expect her to obey him, and that her wild, independent behaviour will cease? Does this make us change our view of the 'new' Benedick – perhaps he is still the old Benedick? Or is this just a throw away line as he kisses her? You decide.

QUICK CHECK

1. Several challenges are made to Don Pedro and Claudio in Scene 1. Who makes these challenges?
2. What is Claudio's initial response to Benedick, when he challenges him?
3. What piece of news does Benedick give Claudio and Don Pedro as he leaves?
4. What does Leonato demand Claudio and Don Pedro do as penance for their treatment of Hero?
5. In Scene 3 how long do Claudio and Don Pedro remain at the monument, paying respect to Hero?
6. In Scene 4, how is Hero's identity kept secret until the last moment?
7. Beatrice and Benedick claim they do not really love each other – how is this shown to be false?
8. How does Benedick stop Beatrice's final joke and mockery?
9. Who enters at the end of the scene?
10. What news does he bring?

The characters

The main characters

Benedick
a young lord of Padua

Beatrice
Leonato's niece

'there is a kind of merry war betwixt Signor Benedick and her' (Leonato, Act 1 Scene 1))

Leonato
Governor of Messina

'…he is no hypocrite, but prays from his heart.' (Don Pedro, Act 1 Scene 1)

Don Pedro
Prince of Arragon

'…I warrant thee, Claudio, the time shall not go dully by us.' (Act 2 Scene 1)

Claudio
a young lord of Florence

'…the right noble Claudio.' (Messenger, Act 1 Scene 1)

Hero
Leonato's daughter

'…she is the sweetest lady that ever I looked on.' (Claudio, Act 1 Scene 1)

The supporting characters

Antonio
Leonato's brother

Don John
Don Pedro's
illegitimate brother

**Friar
Francis**

Conrade   Borachio
followers of Don John

Ursula   Margaret
Hero's maids

Dogberry
a constable

Verges
a headborough
(area watchman)

a Sexton
(like a
magistrate)

Balthasar
Don Pedro's
musical attendant

And...
● **various messengers, watchmen, attendants, and a boy**

Character focus: Benedick

Who is Benedick?

- Benedick is a **gentleman** of **Padua**.
- He is part of **Don Pedro's group** of friends.
- He is a soldier who has **fought alongside Don Pedro** against his enemies.
- He is **Claudio's friend** and mentor.

What does Benedick do in the play?

- Benedick arrives with Don Pedro in Messina (Act 1 Scene 1).
- He claims he will not marry for anything (Act 1 Scene 1).
- Wearing a mask at the ball, he meets Beatrice who insults him (Act 2 Scene 1).
- He is tricked into believing Beatrice loves him (Act 2 Scene 3).
- He starts acting in a lovesick way (Act 3 Scene 2).
- He is present at the ruined wedding and suspects Don John (Act 4 Scene 1).
- He agrees to Beatrice's request that he challenge Claudio (Act 4 Scene 1).
- He challenges Claudio (to a duel) and then leaves angrily (Act 5 Scene 1).
- He marries Beatrice (Act 5 Scene 4).

What does Benedick say and what does this tell us?

Key quotes

> *'it is certain I am loved of all / ladies, only you excepted…'*

(to Beatrice, Act 1 Scene 1)

This shows Benedick's **vanity**; he knows he is **witty**, and it is a constant shock to him that his charms do not appear to work on Beatrice – but it is also why he is intrigued by her.

> *'I will live a bachelor.'*

(Act 1 Scene 1)

Benedick mocks Claudio for showing an interest in Hero, and tells Claudio he intends to remain single for ever.

This adds to Benedick's vanity – he is too good for marriage, or so he believes – and it is his **pride**, **arrogance** and love of **mockery** that make Don Pedro decide to 'set him up'.

> *'…till all / graces be in one woman, one woman shall not come in my grace…'*

(Act 2 Scene 3)

Benedick, in his own way, is a **romantic** – he, too, wants the perfect woman and will not settle for less. Only Beatrice is right for him because she has it all – wit, beauty – and decency (she stands up for Hero's honour).

> *'…Peace I will stop your mouth.'*

(kissing Beatrice, Act 5 Scene 4)

This simple line is important because it shows that wit and clowning can only get you so far. By kissing Beatrice he shows that he has 'grown up' and has learned that actions speak louder than clever words.

What do others say to or about Benedick?

Key quotes

> '...Signor Benedick,
> For shape, for bearing, argument and valour,
> Goes foremost in report through Italy.'

(Ursula, Act 3 Scene 1)

Ursula means there is no one to match Benedick's looks, manners, intelligence and bravery.

Although this is said for Beatrice's benefit (who is hiding) there is a ring of truth in Ursula's words.

Benedick *does* have intelligence and we have already been told at the start of the play that he is:
- a '*good soldier*', and
- has done '*good service*', suggesting he is loyal.

It is unlikely that someone as choosy as Beatrice would fall in love with a man who did not have these qualities.

> '*Why he is the prince's jester, a very dull fool...*'

(Beatrice, Act 2 Scene 1)

Beatrice says this to a disguised Benedick, but it has a ring of truth – Benedick is a clown and makes people laugh. This begins to change when he later reflects upon himself and wonders – is that all I am?

QUICK CHECK

1. Where has Benedick been when he first appears in the play?
2. What is Benedick view about marriage at the start of the play?
3. How does Benedick behaviour change in Act 3 Scene 2?
4. How does Beatrice ask Benedick to prove his love for her?
5. Benedick is a gentleman of which town?
6. At the start of the play how does Benedick think women view him (apart from Beatrice)?
7. Who says that Benedick is just the '*Prince's jester*' (a clown for Don Pedro)?
8. How does Benedick stop Beatrice from talking and mocking him in the last scene of the play?

Look at motives

do brilliantly!

To achieve the highest levels, it is vital that you consider **why characters act as they do**. Sometimes this can lead you to question what you think you know.

For example, is Benedick really that decent?

Let's consider the evidence...
- He **argues** against Claudio's **true love** for Hero – surely not much of a friend!
- He is **tricked into loving** Beatrice – why did he need to be?
- He **challenges** Claudio – yet this is not because it is right, but because he wants the approval of Beatrice.

The point is that when you really examine a character and look at evidence of the motives *behind* their actions you can form new opinions of them.

Character focus: Beatrice

Who is Beatrice?

- Beatrice is **Leonato's niece**, living in Messina.
- She is **Hero's cousin**.
- She is **Benedick's lover** (later in the play – earlier, his 'enemy').

What does Beatrice do in the play?

- When Beatrice hears Don Pedro is arriving (Act 1 Scene 1) she **asks about Benedick** and then **insults him when he appears**.
- She **advises Hero** about men and marriage (Act 2 Scene 1) then **insults a masked Benedick** at the ball.
- Beatrice is **tricked by Hero and Ursula** into believing Benedick loves her (Act 3 Scene 1).
- She **attends the ruined wedding** (Act 4 Scene 1) between Hero and Claudio, and believes Hero has been falsely accused. Beatrice **admits her love** to Benedick, then asks him to **kill Claudio** to prove his love.
- Beatrice **attends the final wedding** (Act 5 Scene 4), masked, and **marries Benedick** – but only after discovered letters have proved their true feelings.

What does Beatrice say and what does this tell us?

Key quotes

Beatrice, like Benedick, says a great deal – but much of it is to **hide her true feelings**.

> *'In our last conflict…'*

(Act 1 Scene 1)

We know from this that Beatrice and Benedick have **already met** – and battled – and she is obsessed with talking about him (even though she insults him).

> *'I had rather hear my dog bark at a crow / than a man swear he loves me…'*

(Act 1 Scene 1)

Beatrice makes it clear she is an **independent** woman who does not want some silly man fawning over her (**but does she mean it**?).

> *'I was born to speak all mirth, and no matter…'*

(to Don Pedro, Act 2 Scene 1)

Beatrice presents herself as the **witty joker**, with no thought of 'serious' things. But note how keenly she gets involved in serious matters later – **defending her cousin**, asking for **Claudio's death**.

> *'Stand I condemn'd for pride and scorn so much?'*

(Act 3 Scene 1)

On hearing Hero and Ursula's words about her, Beatrice shows she **does** care what people think. She, too, **wants to be loved**, as she says:

> *'Benedick, love on, I will requite thee, Taming my wild heart to thy loving hand…'*

(Act 3 Scene 1)

What do others say about Beatrice?

Key quotes

> '...and she were not possessed with a fury, exceeds / her as much in beauty as the first of May doth the last of December.'

(Benedick, comparing Beatrice to Hero, Act 1 Scene 1)

Here, Benedick is admitting that he is **already attracted to Beatrice**. He says that despite her 'fury' she is still much more beautiful than Hero.

> 'By my troth, niece, thou wilt never get thee a husband, if thou / be so shrewd of thy tongue.'

(Leonato to Beatrice, Act 2 Scene 1)

This is the general view: that Beatrice alienates too many men with her **sharp wit**. This **doesn't appear to bother** Beatrice **until later** in the play.

...she cannot love... She is so self-endeared.

> '...nature never framed a woman's heart
> Of prouder stuff than that of Beatrice:
> Disdain and scorn ride sparkling in her eyes,
> Misprising what they look on, and her wit
> Values itself so highly, that to her
> All matter else seems weak: she cannot love,
> Nor take no shape nor project of affection,
> She is so self-endeared.'

(Hero, with Beatrice listening in secret – or so she believes, Act 3 Scene 1)

Hero's speech reveals a lot about Beatrice's character:

- Beatrice's **'scorn'** is **'sparkling'** – it is what makes her such a **character**.
- But she is also **'self-endeared'** – in **love with herself**, like Benedick.
- However, we must remember that **these words are spoken for Beatrice to hear**. Hero wants a reaction from Beatrice who hates to think she is unable to show love.

QUICK CHECK

1. How do we know Beatrice and Benedick have met before?
2. Who is Beatrice's cousin?
3. Who tricks Beatrice into believing Benedick loves her?
4. What does Beatrice demand of Benedick as proof of his love (in Act 4 Scene 1)?
5. How do we know that Benedick finds Beatrice attractive from the start – despite her wildness?
6. What effect do Hero's words about her not being able to love, have on Beatrice?

Remember! In the Shakespeare paper you will be expected to support everything you write by reference to quotations or scenes from the play. Find a quote to support each of your answers.

The domino effect

do brilliantly!

It is important to understand the knock-on effect of what is done and said at various times in the play. Like a line of dominoes, when one is pushed the others follow. For example, when the Watch overhear Conrade and Borachio, the first domino is being pushed over, leading to the truth being revealed.

But, not every action works like this. What about Beatrice's actions? One *could* argue that little of what she does has any effect. She advises her cousin to maintain independence – Hero takes no notice. She demands that Benedick 'kill Claudio' – this proves unnecessary. Finally, her spirited behaviour is stopped by Benedick's kiss. It's his action, not hers.

Character focus: Claudio

Who is Claudio?

- Claudio is a young **lord** of Florence.
- He is a member of **Don Pedro's 'entourage'** (group).
- He is a **soldier** who has **fought alongside Don Pedro** against his enemies.
- He is a **friend** of **Benedick**.

What does Claudio say and what does this tell us?

Key quotes

> *In mine eye she is the sweetest lady that ever I looked on...'*

(Act 1 Scene 1)

Claudio falls **in love with Hero, scarcely knowing her**. But it is a **true love** that cuts through the wit and pretence of Benedick and Don Pedro.

> *'Let every eye negotiate for itself,*
> *And trust no agent: for beauty is a witch…'*

(Act 2 Scene 1)

Claudio clearly does not learn from his own advice (to '*trust no agent*') as he is **easily tricked** by Don John (who says Don Pedro wants to marry Hero).

> *'Bait the hook well, this fish will bite.'*

(Act 2 Scene 3)

Claudio shows his own **love of tricks and games** when 'baiting' Benedick.

> *'She knows the heat of a luxurious bed:*
> *Her blush is guiltiness, not modesty.'*

(Act 4 Scene 1)

Claudio **rejects Hero**, but it is clear that although in **agony**, he has **little judgement and has not grown up** enough to see Hero's virtue for what it is.

> *'choose your revenge yourself,*
> *Impose me to what penance your invention*
> *Can lay upon my sin.'*

(to Leonato, Act 5 Scene 1)

Claudio is now **humble** – he has learnt what life is, and accepts his wrongdoing. The young man who **acted in haste**, now **repents at leisure** (i.e. forever).

What does Claudio do in the play?

- Claudio **falls in love with Hero** (Act 1 Scene 1) and agrees to let Don Pedro woo her on his behalf.
- He **believes** (for a moment) that **Hero loves Don Pedro**, but is soon told the truth (Act 2 Scene 1).
- He is **part of the plan to make Benedick fall for Beatrice** (Act 2 Scene 3).
- He **makes fun** of the lovesick **Benedick** (Act 3 Scene 2).
- He **finds out Hero has been unfaithful** from Don John (Act 3 Scene 2).
- He **rejects** and humiliates **Hero** during their wedding at the church (Act 4 Scene 1).
- He **refuses duels** with **Leonato**, **Antonio** and **Benedick** (Act 5 Scene 1). Then **discovers Hero's innocence**.
- He accepts and carries out his **penance**, holding an all-night vigil for the 'dead' Hero (Act 5 Scene 3).
- Obedient to Leonato, he arrives to marry Leonato's 'niece' but **discovers Hero is still alive**, and **marries her** (Act 5 Scene 4).

> …Choose your revenge yourself;
> Impose to me what penance your invention
> Can lay upon my sin….

What do others say about Claudio?

Key quotes

> He hath borne himself beyond the promise of his age, / doing in the figure of a lamb the feats of a lion.'

(Messenger, Act 1 Scene 1)

Claudio is summed up here – the Messenger points out his **good points** – his **bravery**, his **general behaviour** – but also reminds us **how young** he is.

> 'That young start-up hath all the glory of my overthrow...'

(Don John, Act 1 Scene 3)

The **seeds of Claudio's downfall** are sown here – we find out **Don John is envious** of the way he has been replaced in his brother's affections by Claudio.

> '...I have / known when there was no music with him but the drum and the fife / and now he had rather hear the tabor and the pipe.'

(Benedick, Act 2 Scene 3)

Benedick reflects on the **change in Claudio from soldier to lover** – and mocks it.

> 'Is he not approved in the height a villain...? ...What, / bear her in hand, until they come to take hands, and then with / public accusation, uncovered slander, unmitigated rancour?

(Beatrice, about Claudio's behaviour, Act 4 Scene 1)

Beatrice angrily condemns **Claudio's behaviour** in so **publicly humiliating Hero**, and points out the weakness of the evidence against her – once again exposing Claudio's **youthful lack of judgement**.

QUICK CHECK

1. Who brings news of Claudio's bravery and 'good bearing' in Scene 1?
2. Why does Don John wish to take revenge on Claudio?
3. What does Don John try, *at first*, to make Claudio believe about Hero?
4. How does Benedick think Claudio has changed once he has fallen for Hero?
5. How does Claudio treat Hero at their (first) wedding service?
6. Why?
7. What does Beatrice feel about this treatment of Hero?
8. What penance/punishment does Claudio face for having treated Hero so badly?

More on motives

do brilliantly!

The best students show **insight**. This means looking **beyond the surface** and thinking about why characters act as they do.

Take Claudio. It is easy to say that he feels bad about what he has done. But, does he? When he first admits to his mistake, he asks Leonato to punish him but he also says in Act 5 Scene 1: '...*yet sinn'd I not, / But in mistaking...*' which sounds as if he is excusing himself.

Later, in Act 5 Scene 4, just as Claudio is about to marry Leonato's 'other' niece (a sort of punishment), he is able to swap jokes with Benedick and mock him, saying they will '...*tip thy' horns with gold...*'. The 'dead' Hero doesn't seem much on his mind.

But, remember, Claudio does go through with the penance and seems genuinely moved when he finds out Hero still lives.

I think he thinks upon the savage bull: Tush fear not, man, we'll tip thy thorns with gold...'

Character focus: Hero

Who is Hero?

- Hero is **Leonato's daughter**.
- She is **Beatrice's cousin**.
- She is **Claudio's fiancée**.

What does Hero do in the play?

- Hero is **wooed by Don Pedro** (on Claudio's behalf) at the masked ball (Act 2 Scene 1).
- She **tricks Beatrice** (with Ursula) into believing Benedick loves her (Act 3 Scene 1).
- She **prepares nervously** for her wedding to Claudio (Act 3 Scene 4).
- She **appears at the church to marry Claudio but is rejected** and humiliated by him. She faints (Act 4 Scene 1).
- She is **secretly hidden**, and believed 'dead' by Don John, Don Pedro and Claudio.
- She is **unmasked** at the wedding, and agrees to **marry Claudio** (Act 5 Scene 4).
- She produces **the love letter** or poem proving Beatrice's feelings for Benedick (Act 5 Scene 4).

What does Hero say, and what does this tell us?

Key quotes

Hero says very little in the early part of the play. Claudio sees and falls in love with her based on her looks alone. Act 2 Scene 1 opens with a discussion of marriage. Antonio and Leonato say Hero must do her duty and follow her father's wishes. Beatrice responds for Hero to every question or statement that is aimed at her cousin.

Hero's first proper line in the play is to agree to:

> '…do any modest office…to help my cousin to a good husband.'

(Act 2 Scene 1)

We can imagine Hero's **quiet modesty** here – but not much else – and it is therefore all the more surprising when we see how **full of ideas and intelligence** she is when it comes to tricking Beatrice.

First, she speaks in 'flowery', poetic language – quite a rarity in the play:

> '…bid her steal into the pleachèd bower,
> Where honeysuckles ripened by the sun,
> Forbid the sun to enter…'

(Act 3 Scene 1)

Then in the same scene she speaks with **wisdom** about Beatrice:

> 'I never yet saw man,
> How wise, how noble, young, how rarely featured,
> But she would spell him backward…'

In the first wedding scene, we see her **stunned** and her **innocence shattered** by Claudio's harsh accusations:

> 'Oh God defend me, / how am I beset!

(Act 4 Scene 1)

But by the end of the play (Act 5 Scene 4), she is **serene and dignified**. Claudio has made amends and she is his equal:

> 'One Hero died defiled, but I do live,
> And surely as I live, I am a maid.'

What do others say about Hero?

Key quotes

> *'...it is my cousin's duty to make curtsy, and say,
> 'father, / as it please you'.*

(Beatrice about Hero, Act 2 Scene 1)

Beatrice is pointing out the **basic differences between them**. Hero is a **young, dutiful, modest** daughter. Beatrice is mocking her and reminding her that there is **more to life than 'duty'**.

> *'Silence is the perfectest herald of joy…
> Lady, as you are mine, I am yours…'*

(Claudio to Hero, Act 2 Scene 1)

In contrast to Beatrice and Benedick we hardly hear Claudio and Hero address each other – once again emphasising the youthfulness of their love.

> *'Would you not swear
> All you that see her, that she were a maid,
> By these exterior shows? But she is none.'*

(Claudio, Act 4 Scene 1)

It is clear that Hero **looks modest** and **innocent** and it is this – alongside the sin Claudio thinks she has committed – that he finds so appalling.

> *'But mine, and mine I loved, and mine I praised,
> And mine that I was proud on, mine so much,
> That I myself was to myself not mine...'*

(Leonato, Act 4 Scene 1)

Leonato's **deep love** for Hero – and therefore **distress** at her sin – is shown here. Hero is his own life-blood. Her mother is not mentioned in the play, and **all Leonato's hopes are connected to Hero**, and her future. This love means **he is unable to see clearly** and it takes an **outsider (the Friar)** to see the truth.

QUICK CHECK

1. Who is Hero's father?
2. Who woos Hero on behalf of Claudio at the masked party?
3. Who does Hero speak with in order to trick Beatrice?
4. Why do you think Leonato is especially upset by his daughter's behaviour?
5. What happens to Hero when she is accused at the first wedding?
6. Who suggests that Hero might be innocent?
7. In Act 5 Scene 4, why doesn't Claudio know his bride-to-be is Hero, at first?
8. How does Hero provide proof that Beatrice really does love Benedick?

Develop ideas

do brilliantly!

Students who get lower levels tend to see characters in one-dimensional ways – they are good, or bad, funny or serious, weak or strong. Make sure you **consider all the elements of a character**. For example, it is easy to see Hero as a victim – an uninteresting character who is misused by Don John and Claudio, in different ways.

But surely Hero is not just a victim. She shows real intelligence, wisdom, sparkle – and a good sense of humour – in tricking Beatrice (see her speeches in Act 3 Scene 1). If she lacks anything, it is experience of the big, bad world – but when she is wronged she handles it better than Claudio. When Hero returns from the 'dead', she does so as a complete individual.

> Nothing certainer. One Hero died defiled, but I do live. . .

Character focus: Leonato

Who is Leonato?

- Leonato is **Hero's father**.
- He is **Governor of Messina**.

Key quote

'...if they speak but truth of her,
These hands shall tear her, if they wrong her honour,
The proudest of them shall well hear of it...'

(Act 4 Scene 1)

Leonato's pride – and shame – in his daughter is shown in this quote. **Pride and shame** are closely linked here because Hero owes her father **duty and honour**. This is how a father-daughter relationship worked in those days. By shaming herself, she dishonours her father, to whom she owes so much. Therefore, if she has dishonoured him, Leonato would rather she was dead.

Leonato is very **emotional** here as he had believed his daughter to be faithful and virtuous and cannot bear the thought of what she may have done. However, if she is true, he promises to seek revenge on those who wronged her.

Leonato's role

- Leonarto willingly **welcomes Don Pedro** and his company to Messina (Act 1 Scene 1) and puts on a **masked ball** for the occasion.
- He **instructs Hero to be dutiful** if Don Pedro courts her at the ball (Act 2 Scene 1).
- He willingly **accepts the match between Claudio** and his **daughter** when it comes (Act 2 Scene 1) and is present when the plan to bring Benedick and Beatrice together is made.
- He **takes part in the plot** to trick Benedick (Act 2 Scene 3).
- He is **too busy** with the plans for the wedding **to listen to Dogberry's news** about having captured Borachio and Conrade (Act 3 Scene 5).
- He initially **believes the accusations** against his daughter at the church, and is devastated by them (Act 4 Scene 1).
- He **agrees** that they should **pretend Hero is dead** until the truth comes out (Act 4 Scene 1).
- He **challenges Don Pedro** and **Claudio** to a duel, but they refuse him (Act 5 Scene 1).
- When the truth is revealed about Don John, he **asks Claudio and Don Pedro to do penance** to Hero by attending all night at the 'family monument'. He also instructs Claudio to marry a niece of his (Act 5 Scene 4).
- He **attends the wedding** at which the 'bride' is revealed, and Hero marries Claudio (Act 5 Scene 4).

Character focus: Don Pedro

Who is Don Pedro?

- Don Pedro is the **Prince of Arragon**.

Key quote

> 'I warrant thee, Claudio, the time shall not go dully by us…'

(Act 2 Scene 1)

Don Pedro may be a Prince – and an important man – but he is single, and while he is in Messina he wants to have fun – and forget war. He is at the heart of the plots and games, willingly putting on a mask, and playing a part, but he, too, learns important lessons by the end of the play.

Don Pedro's role

- Don Pedro **woos Hero** on behalf of Claudio – and succeeds (Act 2 Scene 1).

- He **sets in motion** the task of bringing Beatrice and Benedick together (Act 2 Scene 2), and is mainly **responsible for the trick played on Benedick** (Act 2 Scene 3).

- He is also **fooled by Borachio's scheme** to make Hero look impure (Act 3 Scene 2).

- He **supports Claudio's accusations**, and says he is '*dishonoured*' for having linked his '*dear friend to a common stale*' (Act 4 Scene 1).

- But he also **does penance** when Don John's villainy is discovered, and is present at the final wedding scene (Act 5 Scene 4).

Character focus: Don John

Who is Don John?

- Don John is the **illegitimate brother of Don Pedro**.

Key quote

> '…it must not be denied but I am a plain-dealing / villain… let me be that I am, and seek not to alter me.'

(Act 1 Scene 3)

Unlike most of the other main characters, Don John remains a villain – and does not learn or change by the end of the play.

Don John's role

- Don John arrives at Leonato's with his brother, and his friend Borachio (Act 1 Scene 1).

- He is introduced in the first scene, but says he is '*not of many words*'. This is in **direct contrast** with the verbal duelling that has just been taking place between Benedick and Beatrice.

- He **tries to ruin Claudio's relationship** with Hero by telling him Don Pedro intends to marry her (Act 2 Scene 1). This fails.

- He **accepts Borachio's plan** to shame Hero (Act 2 Scene 2).

- He tells **Claudio and Don Pedro about Hero's behaviour** (Act 3 Scene 2).

- He **supports their accusations** at the first wedding (Act 4 Scene 1).

- He is **reported to have fled** (Act 4 Scene 2) and is then reported to have been **caught** (Act 5 Scene 4) but we do not see him again.

4 Key themes

TRICKS AND DECEPTION

> Tricks and deception aren't good things, are they?

> People often deceive others for negative reasons – to trick them out of money, or to make them do something dangerous or unpleasant. But in this play, the tricks and games are generally carried out with the **best intentions** – to make people fall in love; to help someone get what they want; to make someone realise their mistake. Of course, Don John is the notable exception!

> So tricks and deception are good things in *Much Ado*, then?

> Be careful though, not all the deceptions in the play are well meant.

Deception	Reason (if any)
Act 2 Scene 1	
A masked **Don Pedro woos Hero pretending** to be **Claudio** (with his agreement).	▶ Unclear – but perhaps Claudio, being **young and inexperienced**, is afraid he will make a fool of himself.
The masked **Antonio** tries to **trick Ursula** (Hero's maid), but she recognises him; **Benedick**, also masked, tries to speak to **Beatrice**, but she knows it is him; **Don John** tells **Claudio** that **Don Pedro** intends to marry **Hero**.	▶ Most of this is for **entertainment and fun**, but Don John does it out of mere spite.
Act 2 Scene 3	
Benedick is **tricked** by **Don Pedro**, **Leonato**, and **Claudio** (with Balthasar, the singer, present). Benedick thinks he is over-hearing their conversation. They know he is there!	▶ **To make him fall in love** with Beatrice – and see him change from bachelor to love-sick potential husband.
Act 3 Scene 1	
Hero and **Ursula trick Beatrice**. She thinks she is over-hearing their conversation. They know she is there.	▶ **To make her fall in love** with Benedick – and see her change her ways.
Act 3 Scene 2	
Don John tells **Claudio** and **Don Pedro** of **Hero's 'sinful' behaviour**. They go with Don John to seek 'proof'.	▶ Don John is **envious** of Claudio's popularity with his brother.
The planned deception involves **Borachio** being seen with '**Hero**', actually Margaret (Hero's maid), and it looking as if Hero is not as innocent as she seems.	▶ Borachio (who set up the deception) will get **a 1000 ducats** from Don John.

The language of deception: Acts 1 to 3

Act 2 Scene 1
Claudio: *Let every eye negotiate for itself,*
And trust no agent: for beauty is a witch...

Act 2 Scene 3 (song)
Balthasar: *Sigh no more, ladies, sigh no more,*
Men were deceivers ever...

Deception	Reason (if any)
Act 4 Scene 1	
Claudio arrives for the wedding and even **goes through the early part of the ceremony**, before refusing to accept **Hero**, as a result of her 'betrayal'.	▶ Claudio's **pride and honour is hurt**, and he wants to shame Hero and her family.
The **Friar persuades Leonato** to allow people to think that **Hero** is dead.	▶ To **give time for grief and guilt to work on Claudio**. Also, to buy time to find out the truth.
Act 5 Scene 4	
Claudio believes he is to marry a **niece of Leonato's**, but when **Hero** is unmasked, he realises she is alive and willingly takes her as his bride.	▶ Leonato wants Claudio to do **proper penance and be humble**. Also he wants to put him 'on the spot' to see if he still loved his daughter.

The language of deception: Acts 4 and 5

Act 4 Scene 1
(on hearing Hero denounced by Claudio)
Leonato: *Are these things spoken, or do I but*
dream?

Act 5 Scene 1
(confessing to Don Pedro and Claudio)
Borachio: *I have deceived even your very / eyes: what*
your wisdoms could not discover, these
shallow fools / have brought to light...

Well-chosen quotations

do brilliantly!

Choosing a quotation to support a point is vital, but even more impressive is **questioning your own interpretation** by suggesting a **new idea**.

For example, you could say...

'Men are clearly the key tricksters in this play, as Balthasar suggests when he sings 'men were deceivers ever' (Act 2 Scene 3). Take Don Pedro, Claudio, Don John, Borachio and Conrade — to name a few. But what about Hero? She deceives her own cousin, quite willingly. And Margaret must know what she's doing when she pretends to be Hero — even if she doesn't realise how serious it is.'

QUICK CHECK

1. Masks play a large part in the deceptions at the masked ball. How?

2. Both Benedick (in Act 2 Scene 3) and Beatrice (in Act 3 Scene 1) are tricked using the same deception. How are the deceptions carried out?

3. Who pretends to be Hero during Borachio's deception (described in Act 3 Scene 2)?

4. Why is Claudio deceiving everybody at the start of the first marriage scene (Act 4 Scene 1)?

SELF-DECEPTION

So what is the difference between deception and self-deception?

Deception is when someone deliberately misleads or tricks someone else, for any reason. **Self-deception** is when people are deceived about themselves – they fail to see the truth about their own characters, or what is happening to them. Sometimes someone may do this to avoid seeing a painful truth, sometimes because they don't understand themselves. Most of the **deceptions** in this play are caused by others but, in some cases, people are **deceived about themselves**.

Beatrice

On the surface

Beatrice appears to have no interest in pursuing a man or of getting married.

In Act 2 Scene 1 even Don Pedro says of Beatrice:
  '*She cannot endure to hear tell of a husband.*'

And she herself says to Don Pedro:
  '*I was born to speak all mirth, and no matter*'.

Beatrice considers marriage is like a '*Scotch jig*', with passion and speed at the start, but ending with '*bad legs*' and '*repentance*'!

I had rather hear my dog bark at a crow than a man swear he loves me…

In reality

When Beatrice hears Hero's words about her (Act 3 Scene 1) she is shocked:
  '*Can this be true?*
  Stand I condemned for pride and scorn so much?'

She wants Benedick to love her, and reluctantly admits it in Act 4 Scene 1:

Beatrice: *I was about to protest I loved you.*
Benedick: *And do it with all thy heart.*
Beatrice: *I love you with so much of my heart, that none is left to protest.*

By the end of the play she is willingly married.

Benedick

On the surface

In Act 1 Scene 1 Benedick believes all women love him, except for Beatrice.
> '...it is certain I am loved of all / ladies, only you excepted...'

And he goes on to say,
> '...I would I could find in my heart that I / had not a hard heart, for truly I love none.'

By this he means that he wishes he didn't have such a cold attitude to women.

Also in this scene, he also vows that he will '...live a bachelor.' and proceeds to make fun of the love-sick Claudio, little realising what the future holds for him.

In reality

As soon as Benedick believes he is loved by Beatrice, he alters what he said only a short while before.
> 'When I said I would die a bachelor, / I did not think I should live till I were married...
> (Act 2 Scene 3)

When it comes to really serious issues (challenging Claudio), he now despises their foolish jokes. He says to Claudio:
> 'Fare you well, boy, you know my mind, I will leave you now / to your gossip-like humour: you break jests as braggarts do their / blades...'
> (Act 5 Scene 1)

What about the other characters?

Claudio   He is under **the illusion that love is straightforward** – and that the **world of Messina is for fun, laughter and love**. Then Don John's treachery – and his own willingness to believe the worst of Hero – makes him grow up very quickly.

Hero   She, too, has been **protected** in the little world of Messina. She suffers self-deception because she **feels that the world is a kind place that will do her no harm**. When the outer world (in the form of Don John) comes to Messina it damages her and she is changed forever.

Don Pedro   He is deceived by believing he can **control the world around him**. He sets up the love affair between Benedick and Beatrice, and helps arrange Hero and Claudio's marriage – but even he cannot control his half-brother's villainy. He is forced to accept **his error of judgement**, and ask for forgiveness from Leonato.

Leonato   He initially **deceives himself** that his own **daughter** could be capable of **shameful behaviour**. Through his own over-emotional response, we see that he is unable to see the truth. The Friar, Benedick and Beatrice, make him see sense.

QUICK CHECK

1. What illusions does Benedick have about himself?
2. How has the way Benedick speaks changed when he challenges Claudio in Act 5 Scene 1?

More on significant quotations

do brilliantly!

Don John famously says (in Act 1 Scene 3) that '*it must not be denied but I am a plain-dealing villain*'. It is easy to say 'this shows he is a villain'. But, it is **more interesting** to say that he is one of the few characters who is completely true to himself. Remember: **use your insight** to look beneath the surface of key quotations.

LOVE AND MARRIAGE

> **How was marriage different in Shakespeare's time?**

> In those days, marriage was as much a **financial agreement** as anything else. Families needed to make sure that their children married 'well'. Women stayed with their fathers until they were married and it was the responsibility of the father to find the 'right' match for his daughter according to both money and social status.

> **Shakespeare wrote a lot of plays about marriage, didn't he?**

> Yes, marriages can make **great drama** – especially if a girl falls in love with someone unsuitable (think about Romeo and Juliet). In *Much Ado* things go wrong but, as we also see in this play, marriages can also be used to put things right, and to tie up the loose ends, as well as for happy endings!

Relationship: Hero and Claudio

Point	Evidence
Hero and Claudio are both **young**.	▶ In Act 1 Scene 1 Claudio describes Hero as '*a modest young lady*', and Claudio is described as having the '*figure of a lamb*' (figure = appearance).
They are both **'innocent'** in different ways.	▶ Claudio is readily tricked by Don John, and barely questions Hero's guilt. His shock suggests he has never been betrayed before. Hero faints when she is accused in Act 4 Scene 1: she cannot believe her honour has been questioned.
They **hardly know each other** to begin with.	▶ Claudio has seen Hero before he went away to war, but he seems to know little of her: '*Hath Leonato any son, my lord?*' he asks Don Pedro, in Act 1 Scene 1.
They represent the **traditional** way of marriage.	▶ Hero is courted on Claudio's behalf by Don Pedro; then the money side of things is sorted: *...take of me my daughter, and with her my fortunes: his / grace hath made the match*' (Leonato, Act 2 Scene 1). Then Hero and Claudio are formally engaged and (eventually) married.
They are **well-matched**.	▶ Hero and Claudio are both intimately involved in the tricking of Benedick and Beatrice and, in the end, Claudio humbly accepts his penance, and Hero becomes his true equal.

What kind of love?

Hero and Claudio's love is a sort of **adolescent love** – basically, Claudio fancies Hero and she fancies him back. It is a 'visual' love, based on appearances alone. Claudio is a young, brave soldier and a lord; and Hero is an aristocrat's daughter, and beautiful. They **grow up during the play** and their relationship matures and by the time they actually marry it becomes one based on a deeper knowledge of one another.

Relationship: Benedick and Beatrice

Point	Evidence
Benedick and Beatrice **know each other** – there is 'history' between them.	▶ '...there is a kind of merry / war betwixt Signor Benedick and her: they never meet but there's a / skirmish of wit between them'. (Leonato, Act 1 Scene 1)
Theirs is a **modern relationship**.	▶ It could be considered modern, because both are free and can choose (or refuse) whoever they want.
They are **clearly obsessed** (or, at the very least, interested) in each other from the start.	▶ Beatrice's first words in the play are: 'I *pray you, is Signor Mountanto* (meaning Benedick) *returned from the wars or no?*' When they do meet, they quickly slip into insulting each other. (Benedick says: '...*my dear Lady Disdain! Are you yet living?*')
When they do finally fall for each other, it **changes them profoundly**.	▶ Beatrice wants to marry Benedick so much she demands proof of the depth of his love when she asks him to kill Claudio (Act 4 Scene 1). Benedick's agreement to kill a friend shows how much he loves Beatrice.
They are **well-matched**.	▶ Beatrice and Benedick are tricked in the same way. They both hide their true feelings for each other; even when they are about to marry; their pride almost makes them retreat and change their minds. And they love talking to each other – whether it is to insult or show love.

What kind of love?

This is the love of two people who are **well-matched**, and who know each other's faults inside out. If they can stop talking for a minute, they should be happy. It is significant that Benedick 'stops' Beatrice's mouth with a kiss in the final scene!

A bird of my tongue is better than a beast of yours.

Well, you are a rare parrot-teacher

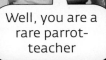

QUICK CHECK

1. Has Claudio seen Hero before the play begins?
2. Claudio is described as having the '*figure of a lamb*'. What does this mean?
3. What are Beatrice's first words in the play?
4. Have Beatrice and Benedick met before?
5. Why does Benedick kiss Beatrice at the end of the play?

Minor characters matter

do brilliantly!

It is tempting to keep to the main characters when you write about key themes and ideas. But don't forget the only other 'love relationship' – the one between **Borachio and Margaret**. Is this simply a plot device (i.e. put in to make the story work) or is Shakespeare saying something about 'lower class' relationships – that they are just a bit of fun?

STATUS AND HONOUR

Status and honour were very important themes in the society of Shakespeare's time and this is reflected in *Much Ado*. **Honour** formed the basis for most relationships in Elizabethan times: the social structure depended on the 'lower' ranks respecting and honouring their superiors, and the family structure similarly depended upon such a code. Fathers owed their daughters safety, protection and sought a suitable marriage for them. In turn, a daughter owed her father respect and was obliged to remain 'virtuous' and 'respectable'.

So what about 'shame' then?

Shame is closely related to status and honour, for anyone not honouring the code brings shame upon themselves and/or their family, regiment or country.

What does the play say about status and honour?

Here are some examples showing where ideas relating to status and honour occur in *Much Ado About Nothing*.

1 **Don John's feeling of rejection** – he feels Claudio has become closer to his brother than him (as an illegitimate 'half-brother' he has little real power, so is 'lower status').

Don John says he is '*...sick in displeasure to him...*' (Act 2 Scene 2).

2 **Claudio owes duty to Don Pedro** because Don Pedro is the Prince and therefore Claudio's superior. Don Pedro initiated the relationship between Claudio and Hero. This is why when Hero is said to have shamed Claudio, it is dishonouring Don Pedro, too.

As Don Pedro says, in Act 4 Scene 1:
'*I stand dishonoured that have gone about
To link my dear friend to a common stale.*'

*stale = prostitute

3 **Leonato feels equally shamed** by his daughter's behaviour, saying:
'*...she is fallen
Into a pit of ink...*'
(Act 4 Scene 1)

4 But, equally, **when she is proved innocent he seeks revenge** on the men who wronged her. So, **too, does Antonio**. The **family honour** has been attacked.
'*God knows, I loved my niece,
And she is dead, slandered to death by villains...*'
(Antonio, Act 5 Scene 1)

5 The **penance** that Claudio and Pedro do, once they discover Hero is innocent, is not just to pray at her 'monument', but, more importantly, to:
'*Possess the people in Messina here,
How innocent she died...*'
(Leonato, Act 5 Scene 1)

*possess = inform

This is to ensure the people know **Hero** (and **Hero's family**) are innocent of any crime or shameful act.

What does the play say about mothers?

- Hero has **no mother**, and Beatrice is **an orphan**.
- Don John is Don Pedro's **half-brother**, but no mention is made of either man's mother.

This lack of mothers – or older women – perhaps makes the women more vulnerable than in other plays. There is no mother to safeguard their interests and no role model. It was very much a 'man's world' in Shakespeare's day, but this absence of mature women shifts the power base: there are no older, high-status women to counteract or dilute essentially 'male' reactions (such as Leonato's anger).

What does the play say about the power of men?

Beatrice's weakness

Being a woman, Beatrice is powerless. She may be very strong in both character and spirit, but she has no real power. We see this when she is unable to take revenge against Claudio's false accusation of Hero. However, Beatrice is able to manipulate the situation by playing to her strengths.

Unable to act herself, she encourages Benedick to do so. She is able to encourage him to use his 'manly' strength, through his love for her.

Were she a man, Beatrice says, she would do it herself.

> *...oh that I were a man for his sake!...'*
> (Act 4 Scene 1)

We get the impression here that Beatrice feels impotent (powerless) being a woman, and frustrated as she finishes the speech with:

> '*I cannot be a / man with wishing, therefore I will die a woman with grieving.*'

Men in charge

In *Much Ado About Nothing* the men are in charge, from organising the initial plan to marry Hero and Claudio, to the false accusation of Hero, to the administering of punishment and finally to the arranging of the 'happy' marriage at the end of the play.

The duties of the daughter are stressed in Act 2 Scene 1, when Antonio (Hero's uncle) still feels it is necessary to remind Hero of her duties:

> '*Well, niece, I trust you will be ruled by your father.*'

However, Beatrice adds her own comment:

> '*Yes faith, it is my cousin's duty to make curtsy, and say, father, / as it please you: but yet for all that, cousin, let him be a handsome / fellow, or else make another curtsy, and say, father, as it please me.*'

Beatrice can say this – Hero cannot. Hero is bound to respect her father. Beatrice may say these things more freely. Luckily for all concerned – Hero seems to feel the same way as Claudio, so all is well.

Remember

- Don Pedro starts the deception of Benedick and Beatrice (with Hero's help, admittedly).
- It is a man – Borachio – who persuades Margaret to help him in the deception.
- Leonato decides Claudio's punishment, and arranges the new marriage.

But... It is Beatrice's utter belief in Hero's decency, supported by the Friar's wisdom, that helps save Hero from shame, and a nunnery. Beatrice is the first to question what has happened:

> '*Oh: on my soul my cousin is belied.*'
> (Act 4 Scene 1)

QUICK CHECK

1. How many mothers appear in the play?
2. What is Beatrice's reaction to Antonio when he says Hero must be dutiful to her father?
3. Who is the first to question whether Hero is really guilty?
4. Why is Don Pedro dishonoured by Hero's behaviour?

Get an overview

do brilliantly!

It is useful to **understand the power structures** in plays.

Take Leonato – he is important as Governor of Messina, but he owes allegiance to the Prince – Don Pedro, of Arragon. This is like the old feudal system of the Lord of the Manor, and his workers.

But how is this helpful in your Test? Suppose you were discussing 'Status and honour'. Think how, at the start of the play, Leonato is polite and courteous to Don Pedro, but once his daughter is shamed by him and Claudio, where do his allegiances lie – with family, or with the Prince?

Use of language

LOTS OF TALK

There is a lot of talking in *Much Ado About Nothing*! People talk about themselves – their love, despair, plans, fears and desires. People talk about other people – what they think, how they might behave, what they have said, what they meant. People also talk a lot for the benefit of others – so that they are overheard, for example.

Examples

- The play opens with a **Messenger telling us** about the imminent arrival of Don Pedro and his company.

- **Benedick and Beatrice's** battle is one of **speech** – there is **no physical violence**!

- **Don Pedro speaks** to **Hero** on **Claudio's behalf**.

- **Benedick** and **Beatrice** fall in **love** because they **overhear others talking** about them.

- **Borachio's plan** depends on others **hearing** him call Margaret 'Hero'.

- **Don John** and **Borachio's villainy** is uncovered by the **Watch overhearing** Borachio boasting to Conrade.

- **Don Pedro** and **Claudio's penance** is to **speak at Hero's monument**, and **inform the people** of Messina that Hero is innocent.

There is a lot of inaction in the play!

Much Ado About Nothing is, in many ways, a play about what *does not* happen. As we know, it is full of illusion, for example:

- Hero is not really unfaithful to Claudio
- Hero does not actually die.

There are, however, some other points of inaction to consider, for example:

- **Wars** and **fighting** take place **elsewhere** (i.e. outside Messina – which is a place of gossip and games)
- The only potential **fight** in the play **does not happen** – Leonato and Antonio challenge Claudio and Don Pedro, but the duel never happens. Similarly Benedick challenges Claudio, but before they can fight, the truth about Hero comes out.

Who does act?

- Ironically, the **man of fewest words** – **Don John** – has the greatest impact on the story. It is his **actions** that almost send the story into tragedy.

- But it is the men who are **least educated**, and **without** the **witty language** of Benedick, i.e. **Dogberry**, and the **Watch**, who **find out the truth**.

- Finally, **Beatrice** and **Benedick's love for each other** is proved not by what they have said (which can be denied) but by **letters and poems** they have **written** – if it is on paper, it must be true!

We see in *Much Ado About Nothing* that talking often arrives only at confusion, deception and inaction. It is characters who are not necessarily good with words (e.g. Dogberry and Verges), and characters who use methods other than language (e.g. Don John), who get the most done!

comment
entertainment
insult   deceit
criticism

Different types of talk

1 Talk is used to **comment about** and '**note**' (observe) others.

Claudio (about Hero):

'In mine eye, she is the sweetest lady that ever I looked on.'

(Act 1 Scene 1)

Beatrice (about Don John):

'How tartly that gentleman looks, I never can see him but I am / heart-burned an hour after.'

(Act 2 Scene 1)

2 Talk is used to **insult**, and **criticise** – both in **fun** and in all **seriousness**.

Beatrice:

'I wonder that you will still be talking, Signor Benedick, / nobody marks you.' (i.e. takes notice of you).

(Act 1 Scene 1)

Leonato to Hero, on hearing she is false:

'Why ever wast thou lovely in my eyes? / Why had I not with charitable hand, / Took up a beggar's issue at my gates…'

(Act 4 Scene 1)

3 Talk is used to **deceive** and **trick**.

Don John (to Claudio and Pedro):

'I came hither to tell you, and circumstances shortened (for / she has been too long a-talking of) the lady is disloyal.'

(Act 3 Scene 2)

4 Talk is used to **amuse** and **entertain**.

Don Pedro (to Beatrice, who is apologising for her jokes):

'Your silence most offends me, and to be merry, best / becomes you, for out a question, you were born in a merry hour.'

(Act 2 Scene 1)

QUICK CHECK

1 Why is speaking essential in the process Beatrice and Benedick fall in love?

2 How does Borachio's talk let him down?

3 Who is the man of fewest words in the play?

4 How is this significant?

5 Dogberry lacks clever speech. Does this matter?

6 What actions prove Beatrice and Benedick's love?

7 Which fights never happen?

Puns and word play

Much Ado About Nothing is full of all sorts of **word-play**. As we have already seen (pages 42–43), nearly all the characters **love to talk** – whatever the reason. Part of that pleasure comes from **playing with language**.

What is a pun?

Someone uses a pun when they use the **same word** (in sound or spelling) to mean different things.

A pun in the title?

The title of *Much Ado About Nothing* is generally believed to contain a pun on the word 'nothing' that might have been pronounced 'noting' in Shakespeare's time. As we have seen, there is lots of 'noting' in the play (i.e. watching and observing).

Puns in the play?

Many of the puns used contain sexual references. These **get laughs** from the audience, but also **suit a play about desire, love and illusion** (after all, puns are a form of illusion – hiding, or revealing their real meanings).

For example, in Act 5 Scene 2, there are lots of references to 'dangerous weapons' ('*fencers*', '*foils*', '*swords*' and '*pikes*') which all have sexual connotations.

In Act 3 Scene 4, Hero says, rather seriously, before her wedding that her '*heart is exceeding heavy.*'. Margaret answers, ''*Twill be heavier soon by the weight of a man*', clearly making reference to the wedding night.

What is word-play?

By word-play we mean, **using words in clever ways**.

In Act 2 Scene 1 Beatrice says she cannot stand 'bearded' men. When it is suggested she marries a man *without* a beard, she gives a quick-witted response:

> '…He that hath a beard is more / than a youth: and he that hath no beard is less than a man: and he that / is more than a youth, is not for me, and he that is less than a man, I am / not for him…'

But it would be a mistake to think that word-play is *always* used deliberately to amuse and entertain. For example, Leonato (speaking about Hero) is able to weave clever language all around the word 'mine', despite the despair he feels.

> 'But mine, and mine I loved, and mine I praised,
> And mine that I was proud on, mine so much,
> That I myself, was to myself not mine,'
> (Act 4 Scene 1)

Give us the swords, we have bucklers of our own.

If you use them, Margaret, you must put in the pikes with a vice, and they are dangerous weapons for maids.

Word battles

Conversations in which people try to **outdo** each other with clever words and insults are central to the play. We see this most notably with Benedick and Beatrice, both before and after they fall in love and even as they are about to be married (Act 5 Scene 4)!

> …come, I will have thee, but by this light I take thee for pity.

> I would not deny you, but by this good day, I yield upon great persuasion, and partly to save your life, for I was told, you were in a consumption.

But other characters also use language to mock and humiliate. For example, Don Pedro, Claudio and Leonato mock the love-sick Benedick in Act 3 Scene 2:

Leonato: *So say I, methinks you are sadder.*
Claudio: *I hope he be in love.*
Don Pedro: *Hang him, truant, there's no true drop of blood in him, to / be truly
            touched with love: if he be sad, he wants money.*
Benedick: *I have the tooth-ache.*

Other **battles of wit** exist between:

- **Benedick**, **Don Pedro** and **Claudio** over Benedick's bachelor life (Act 1 Scene 1).
- **Leonato** and **Beatrice** over her single life (Act 2 Scene 1).
- **Balthasar** and **Margaret** (Act 2 Scene 1) at the masked ball.
- **Hero** and **Margaret** (Act 3 Scene 4) over her wedding preparations.
- **Don Pedro** and **Claudio**, trying to mock **Benedick** (without success), Act 5 Scene 1.
- And even, the **same men** at the start of the final wedding scene (Act 5 Scene 4).

QUICK CHECK

1. How is the title of the play a pun?
2. In Act 5 Scene 4 how are Beatrice and Benedick still playing with words and joking?
3. What word does Leonato repeat several times in clever word-play in Act 4 Scene 1?

Quotations in lists

do brilliantly!

One of the problems with puns and word-play is that students often feel they have to explain every one in great detail. Sometimes it is more effective to use a number of examples to illustrate a point.

For example, you could write:

'Benedick and Beatrice make use of the animal kingdom in their exchanges. Beatrice is a 'parrot-teacher' according to him, but the 'bird of her tongue is better' than his 'beast' according to her; Benedick wishes his 'horse' was as quick as her words, to which she calls him a 'jade' (an old horse!).

IMAGES AND METAPHORS

Much Ado About Nothing is not just a play full of clever language used for wit and insults. It is a play which comes very close to tragedy – and in those moments of danger and despair, characters use powerful images or metaphors.

Who and where	What is said	Meaning
Act 1 Scene 3		
Don John, speaking about himself.	'…I am trusted with a muzzle, and enfranchised with a clog, / therefore I have decreed not to sing in my cage. If I had my mouth, I / would bite…'	Don John compares himself to a **tethered animal**, who is not free to do as he wishes (i.e. 'bite').
Act 2 Scene 1		
Claudio, alone, when he thinks that Hero is to marry Don Pedro.	'Let every eye negotiate for itself, / And trust no agent;:for beauty is a witch, / Against whose charms faith melteth in the blood…'	Claudio believes that **outward appearances** (Hero's beauty) are the work of evil, and **not to be trusted**.
Act 4 Scene 1		
Claudio to Leonato, at the wedding.	'There, Leonato, take her back again, / Give not this rotten orange to your friend…'	Claudio rejects the '*rotten*' fruit – Hero, believing her to have **shamed him** with Borachio.
Leonato, about Hero.	'…she is fallen / Into a pit of ink, that the wide sea / Hath drops too few to wash her clean again, / And salt too little, which may season give / To her foul tainted flesh.'	Leonato mixes two metaphors here – Hero's fall into darkness, (**sin**) which cannot be washed off…and he echoes the food metaphor, by saying that even salt cannot bring flavour (**goodness**) back.
Act 5 Scene 1		
Pedro and **Claudio**, on hearing Borachio admit that Hero is innocent.	Don Pedro: 'Runs not this speech like iron through your blood?' Claudio: 'I have drunk poison whiles he uttered it.'	Don Pedro is suddenly 'weighed down' with this terrible news, but for Claudio, he feels as if the words Borachio speaks are **like poison**, infecting his whole being.

Figurative language (metaphors and similes) is possibly best-suited to moments of dramatic tension and passion because it gives such powerful images and descriptions. However there are plenty of examples of figurative language used in more pleasant circumstances.

Who and where	What is said	Meaning
Act 2 Scene 1 **Beatrice**, speaking to Leonato, Hero and Antonio.	▶ '…hear me, Hero, wooing, / wedding, and repenting, is as a Scotch jig, a measure and a / cinquepace: the first suit is hot and hasty like a Scotch jig (and full as / fantastical), the wedding mannerly modest (as a measure) full of state / and ancientry, and then comes Repentance, and with his bad legs falls / into the cinquepace faster and faster, till he sink into his grave.'	▶ As this is before the masked ball, Beatrice is warning Hero to tackle any approaches from the Prince in a calm fashion – but she then goes on to describe the act of meeting someone, marrying them and then wishing otherwise! Although this is light-hearted, Hero will regret her first wedding – because it all goes wrong before the end.
Act 3 Scene 1 **Ursula** talking with Hero.	▶ 'The pleasant'st angling is to see the fish / Cut with her golden oars the silver stream, / And greedily devour the treacherous bait: / So angle we for Beatrice…'	▶ Ursula describes the act of deceiving someone – and how the pleasure is all in the lead-up – waiting for them to 'take the bait'. Claudio uses a similar metaphor in Act 2 Scene 3 ('Bait the hook well, / this fish will bite.')

Personifying a place

do brilliantly!

Shakespeare gives few stage directions and so the setting of his plays is often ignored by students. But often we can make interesting observations about them.

After all, perhaps the real villain of this play is not a person at all, but a place – Messina! Clearly, it is a town where everyone knows everyone else's business – where gossip and chat, both intentional and unintentional, lead to mix-ups and mischief.

Count the number of times people are overheard in the play. It could only happen in Messina.

Dogberry's use of language

Dogberry's **amusing language** and **behaviour** provides welcome relief among the more serious issues of Acts 3, 4 and 5.

Dogberry's first appearance: Act 3 Scene 3

Dogberry first appears at the start of Act 3 Scene 3. His job is to choose a constable to take charge of the Watch (police). Here, he justifies his choice of one of them: Seacoal. Look at the way he mixes up his words (misusing one word for a similar one). We call these mistakes 'malapropisms'.

He means 'sensible'.

This means 'understand'! Dogberry means 'apprehend' – stop or arrest!

...you are thought here to be the most senseless and fit / man for the constable of the watch: therefore bear you the lantern: / this is your charge, you shall comprehend all vagrom men, you are / to bid any man stand, in the prince's name...'

He means 'vagrant'.

Later, in the same scene, he tells the Watch they must not chat and gossip in the street, and says it is 'tolerable' when he means '*in*tolerable'.

Dogberry's second appearance: Act 3 Scene 5

Once Borachio has been arrested, Dogberry and Verges go to inform Leonato. Again, Dogberry's words get muddled:

- Dogberry misunderstands the word 'tedious' (tiring/dull) and thinks it means 'rich', so ends up insulting Leonato saying he would give all his 'tediousness' to Leonato!

- He says 'odorous' (smelly) when he means 'odious' (unpleasant).

- He again misuses 'comprehended', meaning 'apprehended'.

- He says 'suffigance' instead of 'sufficient'.

- He ends by saying they will proceed with an 'excommunication' when he means 'examination' (questioning of Borachio and Conrade). (If you excommunicate someone, you expel them from their church or religion!)

It is hardly surprising that Leonato takes little notice of Dogberry, and rushes off to prepare for his daughter's wedding!

...if I were as tedious as a king, I could find it in my heart to bestow it all of your worship'

All thy tediousness on me, ah?

Dogberry's third appearance: Act 4 Scene 2

Dogberry takes a leading role in the interrogation of Conrade and Borachio. He is helped by the Sexton and the Watch. However, once again his language gets the better of him:

On arrival at the court Dogberry says:

'Is our whole *dissembly* appeared?'

He means 'assembly' (gathering/group).

'Redemption' means 'forgiveness'! He must mean 'repentance' or 'punishment'.

On finding out what Borachio has done, Dogberry says:

'Oh villain! Thou wilt be condemned into everlasting / *redemption* for this'.

Dogberry also creates laughter when he is called an '*ass*' by Conrade. As the Sexton has already gone, there is no one left to record Conrade's insult. Much to Dogberry's annoyance, he tells anyone who is left:

'But masters, / remember that I am an ass...oh that I had been writ down an ass!'

I am an ass...

Is Dogberry really an ass?

Dogberry's final appearance: Act 5 Scene 1

It is Dogberry's job to reveal the news of Borachio's crime, but no one can understand him. Don Pedro is forced to question Borachio directly. Fortunately, Borachio confesses his crimes in simple and clearly-understood language.

But before Dogberry leaves, he still has time to mangle his words. His very next speech contains three mistakes! He also manages to remind people that he is an '*ass*' and that it needs writing down.

'Come, **bring away the plaintiffs**: by this time our sexton hath / **reformed** Signor Leonato of the matter: and, masters, do not forget / to specify when time and place shall serve, **that I am an ass**.'

Comment on effects not just actions

do brilliantly!

It is easy to get a satisfactory level in the Test by writing about what **Dogberry** does, and its comic effect on the tone of the play, but really **good answers** will **say more**. He is a comic figure – rather pompous and full of himself – and he uses language he does not really understand. But it is he, and the other less educated men, who reveal Borachio's crime.

In this sense, one might argue Dogberry has more impact on the **outcome** of the play than, say, Benedick or Beatrice.

QUICK CHECK

1. What are 'malapropisms'?
2. How does Dogberry accidentally insult Leonato in Act 3 Scene 5?
3. Why is Dogberry so keen that people remember he is an 'ass'?
4. Why is Don Pedro forced to question Borachio himself?

1 Understanding the question

'Understanding the question' sounds easy enough, doesn't it? However, in the Test, you have to be especially careful that you understand **exactly what you have to do**. If you do not, you will **not** be answering the question and your mark will be low.

What do I have to do in the Test?

In the Test you have to produce a continuous piece of writing on *Much Ado About Nothing* for the **Shakespeare Paper**. This means you have to write on **two scenes** from the play. The question will link these two scenes together and you must **write about both scenes** in your answer.

For example:

> **Much Ado**
>
> Act 1 Scene 1
> Act 4 Scene 1
>
> **What different impressions do we get of Claudio in these two extracts?**

What is this question asking?

You will find that it is a lot easier to understand what a question is asking you to do if you break it down first.

You may already have your own way of breaking down a question, but the following process is good practice for the Test.

Key words	Conclusions	Action
Highlight the key words from the question. In this case: • 'What' • 'different impressions' • 'we' • 'Claudio' • 'two extracts'.	From these key words we can conclude: • This is a question about character and behaviour (Claudio's) and how it comes across to the audience ('we'). • It is also suggesting that Claudio is 'different' in the two extracts. This difference could be: in his behaviour/actions, or in his relationship to other characters (i.e. Hero).	What you do with these conclusions in the Test: • Write about Claudio mainly – what impression we get. • Write about other characters only in their relationship to Claudio. • Look at how he is different in the two scenes or how he changes/develops.

What will the Test question be about?

In the Test, the *Much Ado* question will target one of the following areas:

The sample question on page 50 targets **Character and motivation**. The question looks at Claudio's **character**. **How** it changes is related to **motivation** – why he acts as he does.

▶ Character and motivation
▶ Ideas, themes and issues
▶ The language of the text
▶ The text in performance

Here are two more examples of Test questions:

1

Act 1 Scene 3
(Don John, Conrade and Borachio)
Act 3 Scene 2
(Don John talking to Don Pedro and Claudio)

How would you **perform** the part of **Don John** in these two scenes to bring out his **character**?

- 'How' suggests the way something occurs or is shown.
- 'Perform' tells us we are being asked to advise on the acting of a character's behaviour (performance).
- 'Don John' means we must focus on what this character says and does.
- You will need to look for character clues in these two scenes.

2

Act 1 Scene 1
(Benedick's arrival)
Act 2 Scene 1
(The masked ball)

How do **Benedick** and **Beatrice** use **language** to **hide what they really feel** in these **two extracts**?

- 'How' suggests the way something occurs or is shown.
- The question mentions two characters – so keep to them and them alone.
- 'Language', is the examiner's focus. The question is asking how these two characters speak, what they say and how this is different to what they feel.
- You will need to find evidence in the two extracts.

TIP

When you are responding to a question on character performance (as with Question 1 above), be aware of the fact that there may be several aspects to the same character.

For example, in Question 1, you would probably want an actor to bring out Don John's devious and villainous side. But, try to resist seeing characters as one-dimensional – are there any other sides to the character?

Don John also reveals a more vulnerable and hurt side when Claudio is shown more favour than him. You would need to include points such as this in order to create a balanced picture of the character you are discussing.

QUICK CHECK

Look at the question below.

Act 1 Scene 1 and
Act 4 Scene 1

What different impressions do we get of Leonato in these two scenes?

- Which of the four skill areas is this question looking at – **character and motivation, ideas, themes and issues, the language of the text, the text in performance**?
- Highlight the key words and decide what the question is asking you to do.

2 Finding and using evidence

Evidence is one thing that you **must never forget** when writing about *Much Ado About Nothing*, or any text. **Without evidence**, you have **no proof** for the things you say and your answer is really not worth very much. Using evidence in your answer means that you quote from the text and refer to the text in order to support the points that you make.

Finding evidence for your answer

Let's look at a sample Test question and see **how** you go about finding the quotes you need.

The table below contains the evidence about **Leonato** that you can find in **Act 1 Scene 1**.

> Act 1 Scene 1 and
> Act 4 Scene 1
>
> **What different impressions do we get of Leonato in these two extracts?**

Focus	Evidence	Impressions given
How Leonato acts	Leonato enters reading a letter in which he learns that Don Pedro and his company are coming to Messina that night.	Leonato is **interested** in the people who are about to arrive – **excited** perhaps?
What Leonato says	Leonato says he prefers to bring pleasure rather than pain: '*How much better is it to weep at joy, than to joy at weeping!*'	This shows he **likes to see people happy** – and dislikes getting pleasure from others' unhappiness.
	Leonato welcomes Don Pedro and his company with elaborate praise: '*...when you depart from me, sorrow abides...*' He then exchanges light-hearted talk with Don Pedro. He even welcomes Don John who has a bad reputation.	Leonato **knows his duty**, but is also able to make jokes and enjoy Don Pedro's company. This shows a man at ease with things – happy with the world and what it will bring. He also welcomes Don John, preparing to trust him and show him honour.
How others act and speak towards him	Don Pedro tells Hero that Leonato is an '*honourable father...*' and takes Leonato's hand as they exit in order to enter the house.	Leonato is a man who is **worthy of respect**, both as a father and the Governor of Messina.

> Let me bid you welcome, my lord, being reconciled to the prince your brother: I owe you all duty.

Look at what evidence there is about **Leonato** in the second scene: **Act 4 Scene 1**.

Focus	Evidence	Impressions given
How Leonato acts	▶ Leonato is keen for the wedding to begin. He has also just arrived from the previous scene where he was too busy and flustered to listen to Dogberry.	▶ Leonato is **too tied up in his own family's business and happiness**. As the proud father he does not see the warning signs.
What Leonato says	▶ Leonato answers for Claudio, expecting him to have no objections to marrying Hero: *'I dare make his* (Claudio's) *answer, none.'*	▶ This shows how **trusting** Leonato is. And how sure he is that things are going well.
	▶ When his daughter's sin is revealed Leonato says: *'Hath no man's dagger here a point for me?'*	▶ Could this show Leonato is **more worried about his family honour**, than about his daughter's feelings? It shows how **deeply he is wounded by what has happened**.
	▶ Leonato makes a long speech about Hero as a baby and child: *'…mine I loved, and mine I praised…'*	▶ This long speech is about how Leonato has **worshipped and loved Hero** since her birth. But it also shows how **hurt he is by the accusations**.
What others say	▶ Don Pedro tells Leonato that he (Don Pedro) is *'dishonoured'* by what has happened.	▶ This could create the impression that Leonato is, in his own way, **guilty**. After all, he is the one who produced the daughter who has shamed the Prince (Don Pedro) and Claudio.

TIP

Remember that it is **very bad style** just to list quotes in your writing. The evidence (quotes) needs to be a part of your writing and not just 'stuck in' because you have been told that you need to quote!

This formula is very useful to remember:

- **P**oint: Make a statement.
- **E**vidence: Quote your evidence from the text to support your point.
- **E**xplanation: Expand on your point with reference to the evidence you have used.

This is a **fool-proof way of making sure that you use evidence correctly**.

Point, Evidence, Explanation

Using evidence in your answer

You need to be careful that the evidence you select is **useful** and **valid** for the question you are answering. In this question, you are being asked to discuss the **impressions of Leonato**, not Hero or Claudio. **Any reference to these characters needs to be in relation to Leonato** and the impression we get of **him**.

There are different ways of using evidence. You do not **always** need to quote the text directly. Sometimes you can **paraphrase** or **summarise** what a character says to show what he/she is feeling/thinking. Here are two ways of expressing the same information.

Paraphrasing and summarising

Paraphrasing or **summarising** means stating what has happened or what a character has said, felt, or shown in **your own words**.

Example:

> Leonato is devastated by the news of his daughter's sin, and appears to prefer her dead, rather than for her to live in dishonour.

Direct quotation

A **direct quotation** means putting into your answer the **exact words** said by a character.

Example:

> Leonato tells everyone that 'Death is the fairest cover for her shame...' showing that he wishes his own daughter were dead.

Here, 'Death is the fairest cover for her shame...' are **the actual words from the play** (said by Leonato in Act 4 Scene 1). Note that they have been put into inverted commas/speech marks to show that these are **not** the student's words.

There is more on both **paraphrasing** and **using direct quotations** in the next unit on pages 56–59.

QUICK CHECK

There are **three** pointers used in the tables on pages 52 and 53:
1 how a character behaves
2 what they say
3 how others act and speak towards them

Take **any one** of these pointers, and make a note of the impression this evidence gives of the **Friar** in **Act 4 Scene 1**. Use both skill areas (paraphrasing and direct quotation) when using evidence in your answer.

Levels of evidence

Sticking to the **P.E.E. rule** is a good way to make sure that you use evidence correctly. However, you should consider the **level guide** below so that you use evidence in the best way possible for **maximum marks**.

Lower level evidence

You will get a lower Test level if:

- **you do not provide any evidence** for your opinion at all

- you include quotations but just **copy** them and **do not offer a reason** for including them.

> Leonato is really upset by what happens.

> This essay is about Leonato. He says 'she is fallen into a pit of ink...'

Medium level evidence

You will only get a medium level if:

- you include quotations – in support of what you say – but **do not really develop your ideas (expansion)**. You might pick on a key line or dialogue but only say something very basic and obvious about it.

> In this scene, Leonato says he wishes his daughter were dead. He tells those present that '...Death is the fairest cover for her shame...'

Higher level evidence

To get the highest levels:

- the evidence you select needs to be **relevant and really support what you want to say**.

- you take the evidence you have mentioned and either **link it to supporting evidence**, or use it to **contrast** with **other points** you are making.

- you provide **further explanation** or **offer possibilities** as a result of the evidence.

do brilliantly!

> The **impression** given of Leonato in Act 4 Scene 1 is of a man who is thoroughly devastated by his daughter's apparent crime, speaking of her 'foul tainted flesh...' and unable to see the truth in her innocence, blinded as he is by her sin.
>
> This **same man** has degenerated from the proud father in Act 1 Scene 1, where he was full of the joy of welcome to one who **gives the impression he will never know happiness or trust again.**
>
> But are his words just hot air? After all, following his angry words he is persuaded by the Friar, and is soon vowing that if Don Pedro and Claudio have '...**wrong her honour, The proudest of them shall well hear of it...**'

Paraphrasing, summarising

As mentioned in Unit 2 (page 54), there are different ways of writing down the points you want to make, using evidence from the play. These different methods include paraphrasing, summarising and quoting.

Imagine you have been asked this question in the Test:

> Act 4 Scene 1 and
> Act 5 Scene 1
>
> **How is the theme of family honour developed in these two scenes?**

How to paraphrase the dialogue

One way of making your points is to **paraphrase** what is said. This means putting actual lines and details from the play into your own words.

> …Thou hast kill'd my child, If thou kill'st me, boy, thou shalt kill a man.

> He shall kill two of us, and men indeed, But that's no matter, let him kill one first; Win me and wear me…

Here are some examples of **good paraphrasing** from Act 5 Scene 1. Note how a good paraphrase finds a **different way** of saying the information, but it keeps the **tone** of the original quote.

The facts and the dialogue Act 5 Scene 1	Paraphrase
Leonato and Antonio confront Don Pedro and Claudio about the 'death' of Hero before demanding a duel Leonato: *Thou hast so wronged mine innocent child and me, / That I am forced to lay my reverence by…*	As Leonato meets Don Pedro and Claudio he accuses them of treating his **guilt-less daughter** and himself so badly that he will **no longer show honour** to the Prince but, instead, must challenge his 'superior' to a duel.
And later Antonio: *…I loved my niece; / And she is dead, slandered to death by villains…*	Antonio supports his brother because of his love for his niece **Hero**, and also accuses Don Pedro and Claudio of making a **false accusation**.
Don Pedro replies: Don Pedro: *…My heart is sorry for your daughter's death: / But on my honour she was charged with nothing / But what was true, and very full of proof.*	When Don Pedro replies he says he does feel **sympathy** for Leonato **in his loss**, but **swears** that Hero was only accused of something for which she was guilty and for which there was much **evidence**.

and using quotations

TIP

In order to paraphrase effectively you need to:

1 Know the facts

Be clear about what is going on so you can you put the action and ideas into your own words.

In the examples of paraphrasing in the table on page 56, it is clear that:

- Leonato and Antonio believe that both Don Pedro and Claudio are guilty of slandering Hero, and therefore dishonouring her and them.
- Claudio and Don Pedro believe they know the truth about Hero's guilt – and have seen the proof with their own eyes. They believe that their honour has to be maintained.

2 Find words that are close in meaning to the original ones

Here are some of the alternative words found by the student in the example on page 56:

Original words or phrases	Paraphrase
'...mine **innocent child**...'	'*innocent*' = guilt-less '*child*' = daughter
'...**lay** my **reverence by**...'	'...*lay by*' = put to one side, not do any longer; '*reverence*' = honour
'...very full of **proof**...'	'*proof*' = evidence

How to summarise the action

Examiners **do not** want to see you simply re-telling the story of *Much Ado About Nothing*. If you have to summarise, do so in **clear, fluent** explanations.

Low level summary

The whole explanation is **too long**. If you are going to summarise what happens **make it short**! For example, **all the names are mentioned** unnecessarily.

'*badly*' is **too general** – you need to sum up their behaviour more powerfully (i.e. 'defiled' her, or 'destroyed' her).

Too chatty and informal. This is slang! It also doesn't give the sense of the depth of Leonato's feelings.

> Leonato and Antonio meet with Don Pedro, the Prince, and Claudio, the young lord, and they say that Pedro and Claudio have treated Hero really badly, which is true, and that this isn't good for Leonato's family or for Hero herself. They get well annoyed but Don Pedro and Claudio won't fight with them as they think they know Hero is guilty which she isn't.

Higher level summary

do brilliantly !

This is a single paragraph summary, precise and to the point.

These words mean the names do not have to be repeated.

This neat phrase sums up how Antonio and Leonato believe Hero has been treated.

This summary description replaces a longer explanation about how Claudio and Pedro might feel about Hero's guilt being challenged.

> Leonato and Antonio confront Don Pedro and Claudio and accuse them of piling unfair dishonour and shame on Hero. But the Prince and his companion decline the older mens' challenge to fight, confident of Hero's guilt.

How to use quotations

A quotation is when you include the exact words said by a character in the play in order to make a point. It is important that you quote **regularly** and **relevantly** in your Test answer. Also, remember that **you must ALWAYS use speech marks when you quote from a text**.

Look at this sample Test question:

> Act 1 Scene 1 and
> Act 4 Scene 1
>
> **How does Shakespeare use language to show the contrast between the way Claudio first perceives Hero and how he looks at her later?**

TIP

Do not forget
P. E. E.:

Point, **E**vidence,
Explanation.

Now look at one section from a student's answer. Look at **how** the quotation has been used and placed in the student's answer.

- The student makes the point first (about the simple, innocent view of Hero).

- Direct quotation from Claudio is used to support the initial point.

- The student then goes on to provide comment on the quote that has been used.

> In Act 1 Scene 1 Claudio describes Hero in simple, plain language. He has an innocent view of her. Although his speeches are short, he is clearly moved by her:
> 'Can the world buy such a jewel?'
>
> By comparing her to a jewel, Claudio shows that he has been struck by Hero's beauty. His comments are flattering and highlight that he feels she is special, but he does not know her yet.

In mine eye, she is the sweetest lady that ever I looked on.

In simple terms, the structure of the student's comment looks like this:

The STUDENT'S WORDS start the point being made.	→	SHAKESPEARE'S quotation(s) in speech marks provide evidence.	→	The STUDENT'S WORDS comment on the quote to support the point being made.

Other ways of using quotations

1 Lists of linked words

Sometimes, rather than quoting a whole line, or part of a line, you might want to focus on individual words. Look at this example, answering the same question as on page 58:

> In Act 4 Scene 1 Shakespeare uses language to paint a clear picture of Hero's sinful behaviour with characters calling her, at various points in the scene, a 'rotten orange', 'an approved wanton', and a 'common stale'.

Note how the student puts each individual word or phrase into separate sets of inverted commas to reflect the fact that these are said at different times in different speeches in the scene.

Putting the quoted words together like this gives really clear evidence to support the point being made.

2 Longer quotations

Try to avoid these, unless you are able to comment on the whole section you have included. If not, the Test marker may assume you are simply trying to fill the page.

Here is a good example from the same answer:

do brilliantly!

> In Act 4 Scene 1 Leonato's language makes his own feelings of despair and shame especially clear when he says:
>
> > 'Why ever wast thou lovely in my eyes?
> > Why had I not with charitable hand,
> > Took up a beggar's issue at my gates,
> > Who smirchèd thus, and mired with infamy,
> > I might have said, no part of it is mine.'
>
> This really does show how strongly Leonato feels, in that he claims an adopted beggar's child would have been preferable to Hero, as he could have at least claimed it had no blood of his if it had shamed him in the same way.

The point is made by the student.

The quotation is placed apart as it is a longer one.

A comment on what is meant by the quotation is added.

QUICK CHECK

Here is a line said by Claudio in Act 4 Scene 1 about Hero:

'Would you not swear /
    All you that see her, that she were a maid*...?'   (*maid = innocent, virginal young woman)

Put part of this quotation into a statement about how Hero is described by others in this scene. Start with: It is clear that Claudio wants to point out...

4 Structuring your answer

The **structure** is the **order** and the **sequence** that you use when you write your answer. The structure is not **what** you say (i.e. the themes and ideas) but **how** you put your ideas across, the argument you develop.

You need to think about **how** you answer a Test question **before** you begin writing. Think about it this way: you want to make a cake, and you may know how you want the cake to taste, but if you do not follow the recipe, and add the ingredients in the right order, you may not end up with a cake at all, you may end up with a complete mess! It is the same with writing essays. So, always **think structure, or your argument may fall apart!**

Look at this fairly typical Test question:

> Act 2 Scene 1 and
> Act 4 Scene 1 (end: Beatrice and Benedick alone)
>
> **What impression do we get of Beatrice in these two extracts?**

What approach am I going to take in order to answer this question in the best way?

There are **two** ways you can approach answering such questions:

Approach 1

Write about **each scene in turn** in relation to the **subject** of the question.

Structure

- Introduction
- First scene – points
- Second scene – points
- Conclusion

Advantages

- Easy-to-follow
- Clear and straightforward to read.

Disadvantages

- You might end up just retelling what happened and not analysing.
- It can be difficult to link ideas and draw comparisons with this approach.

Approach 2

Take the **subject** of the question and write about **each point in turn** in relation to each scene.

Structure

- Introduction
- First point – relevant to each scene
- Second point – relevant to each scene
- Third point – relevant to each scene
- Conclusion

Advantages

- Possibly more interesting
- Less danger of just retelling the story.

Disadvantages

- More complicated
- Jumping between scenes can be difficult.

How do I use these structures in my writing?

Take a look at the sample question on page 60 .
This is how you would answer this question using both approaches.

Approach 1

Using this approach, you would **deal with each scene in turn**. You would discuss all the impressions of Beatrice in the first scene before moving on to discuss the impressions we get of the same character in the second scene.

Act 2 Scene 1
- **Quick-witted** – especially with Benedick
- **Sharp** – especially with Benedick
- **Independent** – has a poor view of men, especially as husbands

Act 4 Scene 1 (end)
- **Ready for love** – prepared to show her feelings
- **Prepared to rely/depend upon a man** – she asks Benedick to avenge Hero's false accusal
- **Still fiery** – wants to have Claudio killed

Finally, you would conclude your answer by making comparisons between the impressions of Beatrice in the two scenes and commenting on any differences or similarities.

Approach 2

With this approach, you **deal with each point in turn**. You would discuss a point in relation to both Scene 1 and 2 before moving on to the next point and doing the same with that.
- **Her feelings about love/husbands** – you would write about how this is shown in **both scenes**.
- **Her quick-wit and sharp tongue** – how this is shown in the **first** scene but less so in the **second**.
- **Her developing relationship with Benedick** – how this is shown in **both scenes**.
- You would **conclude** in a similar way to Approach 1 – by making comparisons and commenting on differences and similarities between the impressions of Beatrice in the two scenes.

Which approach (1 or 2) do you think the following student is using?

One of the impressions we get of Beatrice in Act 2 Scene 1 is her utter refusal to consider loving a man as a husband, saying that love and marriages are like 'Scotch jigs' and end up with a furious dance and 'repentance' (regret) at the end. She also has some harsh words to say about Benedick:

> '...he is the Prince's jester: a very dull fool only his gift is, in devising impossible slanders: none but libertines delight in him, and the commendation is not in his wit, but in his villainy, for he both pleases men and angers them, and then they laugh at him and beat him...'

Here Beatrice portrays Benedick as being quite surplus and unimportant, saying that he has few talents and others only laugh at him. However, looking at the same issue — Beatrice's views about men (and Benedick in particular), we can see that things seem to have changed by Act 4 Scene 1. Now, Benedick is the 'man' who can put things right, by killing Claudio and proving his love for Beatrice. Now she wants Benedick's approval — and his love.

This is a **successful answer** because:

- it **compares** one aspect of Beatrice's character across two scenes
- the student has used **explanation** and **connectives** to link to the second scene.

Have a look through the answer again and see if you can spot these elements.

How to use sentences and paragraphs to organise your ideas

How can I grab the attention of the examiner? I want him to notice *my* work!

Whichever approach you use, a well-structured paragraph can make the points you wish to make crystal clear. Remember, it is not just the **overall structure** that is important, you also need to consider carefully the structure of **each paragraph**.

For good paragraph structure you can use the topic sentence (often the first sentence of a paragraph) to make the main point. As you see in this example, you then expand upon the topic sentence, using evidence, in the rest of the paragraph:

The first sentence here gets the key point across. This is why it is called the topic sentence. It uses a word from the question title ('impression') and then says what that impression of Beatrice is (she is sharp-tongued).

The second sentence provides the evidence to support the main point made in the first sentence. It is in this sentence that the student expands on the key point.

> One of the impressions we get of Beatrice is how sharp-tongued she is. For example, in Act 2 Scene 1 she sums up Don John in one quick description saying she gets 'heart-burned' one hour after seeing him!

TIP

Style is also essential when writing an answer to a Test question. It is important that you use interesting **connectives** when linking ideas together. In the student's answer above, the phrase 'For example,' **links (or connects)** the **topic sentence** (the main point) and the **evidence**. To make your writing interesting, try to vary the way you link points and evidence together.

Instead of using 'for example' you could try:
- 'This can be seen when...' or 'This is shown in...' or 'We see this in...'

*do **brilliantly**!*

Higher level sentences

To get a higher mark, you need to attract the Test marker's attention. Try constructing paragraphs in more imaginative ways. Make interesting and valid points about the text. Remember, the Test marker will have read hundreds of answers – make yours stand out.

Look at this example.

> Witty, sharp-tongued and independent are three words we can use to sum up the impression we get of Beatrice in Act 2 Scene 1, but what evidence is there for this?

Note the **structure of the sentence**: starting a paragraph with a **pattern of three adjectives** is very memorable. This is not a style that basic answers would use.

The **rhetorical question** at the end of the paragraph is impressive. Why? Because *you* are going to answer your own question. It is like a trailer for your answer, it gives a clue about what you are going to say, it opens the debate.

Structuring your answer – a summary

In order to answer the question successfully you need to:

- **answer** what **the question** asks

- **support** what you write with **evidence**

- **structure** your answer in a **clear** and **logical** way

- **use a variety of connectives**

- **vary** your use of **sentence structure** so that your answer is individual.

do brilliantly!

Don't forget

- Write about **BOTH** scenes.
  (Your essay needs to be **balanced** and if you only write about one scene you are not answering the question. Many students fall down here and their marks suffer as a result.)
- **Time yourself** so that you have enough time to write all your points on both scenes.
- **Leave about half the time** for the second scene if you are following **Approach 1**.
- **Divide your time equally** over your individual points, if you are following **Approach 2**.
- **Do not rush any section**, plan your time.
  (It is natural that **you might have more to say about one scene** than another, so the amount you write **need not be identical**.)
- **Focus your attention where it is needed.** Do not spend too long on one point but **balance the focus of the discussion**.
- **Do not** refer to **other scenes** or elements in the play **unless** it is helping you to make a point about the scenes you have been given. If you do not explain **why** you have referred to another scene and **why it is relevant to the question**, it is just useless information. You need to **link** the reference to the question.

The plan

To help you avoid missing out anything important, you need to allow yourself **5 minutes from the 45 you are given** to plan your answer. **This is essential.**

Try to write down words and phrases as prompts and then put them into a logical order. Decide on the order **before** you begin writing – you may find it helps to number the paragraphs.

When you have a plan to follow, you can decide how long you need to spend on each section – and stick to it! You need to make timing yourself to write Test answers a part of your Test practice.

Intro	para 1
<u>Act 2 Scene 1</u>	
Witty	para 2
Independent	para 3
Sharp-tongued	para 4
<u>Act 5 Scene 1</u>	
Less concerned with wit	para 5
Relies on a man	para 6
Conclusion	para 7

QUICK CHECK

In three minutes, try to write down adjectives (up to six in total) to describe Beatrice in Act 3 Scene 1 and Act 5 Scene 4. Then write paragraph numbers next to each one to decide which order/priority you would use them to write about her.

5 Writing about two scenes

Yes, yes, I MU
plan, but ho

In this section, we are going to look at how to go about putting together all the ideas you have within a time limit. In the Test you will have to answer on **two scenes** and, as we saw in Unit 4, the most straightforward way to do this is to **write about each scene in turn**. However, to get **maximum marks, you must plan your answer**.

Planning the points

Here is an expanded plan of some points a student wants to make in answer to a question about the **impressions we get of Benedick in Act 1 Scene 1, and at the end of Act 2 Scene 3**. Practising with this format will help you to prepare a more concise plan in the Test.

Introductory paragraph: basic action/background

- **Act 1 Scene 1** – Benedick arrives, ready to swap jokes and insults with Beatrice and offer his views on marriage and women.
- **Act 2 Scene 3** – Benedick reflects on what he has heard about himself and vows to love Beatrice and change his ways.

Section on Act 1 Scene 1: points in order of importance

Impressions of Benedick

- **Single** and **independent** – when Claudio says he loves Hero, Benedick says he '*will live a bachelor*'.
- **Vain** – Benedick says to Beatrice he is '*certain I am loved of all ladies, only you excepted...*' and says only a real '*earthquake*' will make him 'quake' with love for a woman.
- **Rude** and **insulting** (but in a joking way?) – Benedick says that he can see '*without spectacles*' and that he sees '*no such matter*' (when asked if Hero is the '*sweetest lady*' ever seen).

Section on Act 2 Scene 3: points in order of importance

Impressions of Benedick

- **Humble?** – Benedick says that he '*must not seem proud*', and he fears the '*censure*' (criticism) of others.
- **Foolish and two faced?** – Benedick makes excuses about the things he has said earlier, saying that it is possible for a man to change ('*doth not the appetite alter*') and that when he said he would '*die a batchelor*' he just meant he would die young before he had the chance!
- **Interested in love** – he says '*love me? Why it must be required*'.

Conclusion

The **original Benedick** that we meet in Act 1 Scene 1 is witty and independent, although vain. By Act 2 Scene 3 we see him start to **develop** into a more humble man, able to show love but suddenly less sure of himself. But if we take Benedick's earlier comments at face value, his sudden 'about face' could be argued to be hypocrisy.

Planning an essay in this way gives you a solid structure in which to make your points, but you need also to take care about **how** you express yourself. Your paragraphs need to be joined together logically, as do the ideas within each paragraph, otherwise your answer will not 'flow'.

Linking ideas within and between paragraphs

It is absolutely vital that you use connecting words and phrases to organise your writing. Learn what each of these **key connectives** means, and use them to make your points crystal clear.

Key connectives	Purpose	Meaning	Example
Firstly Then Secondly Later Finally	For sequence	To show the order in which events or processes occurred.	*Firstly*, Benedick reflects on what he has heard, *then* when Beatrice enters, he puts his thoughts into action.
In the same way Similarly Also too Likewise	For comparison	To show similarities between ideas.	*In the same way* that Beatrice is surprised to be criticised, so *too* Benedick is surprised to hear others say he would deal 'proudly' with any expressions of love.
Moreover What is more In addition Exactly	For development or emphasis	To make a further point to support an idea.	*Moreover*, Benedick decides that it is quite natural to change (and his ideas were not fixed anyway!).
On the other hand In contrast However But	For contrast	To show differences between ideas.	*In contrast* to Act 1 Scene 1, in the second scene, Benedick is now less sure of himself.
On the whole In conclusion To conclude Finally Overall To sum up Ultimately	For conclusion	To summarise and reflect on what has been written or discussed.	*Ultimately*, at the end of the play, Benedick shows himself capable of real love and friendship with Beatrice.

TIP

For a **higher level** in the Test, you are required to explain and develop your ideas fully. You need to **demonstrate** that you are **expanding** on a point. If you use phrases such as **'What is more'** and **'In addition'** you are making it obvious to the marker that you have taken an idea and developed it.

Model answer

Looking at a model answer is a good way to improve your own skills. If you study the following response – break down the information, look to see **what** the student has done and **how** it has been done – you will find it much easier to be in control of your own writing.

This example deals with the **first** part of the answer, which contains:

- the **introductory paragraph**
- the first section on **Act 1 Scene 1**.

do brilliantly !

Opening paragraph sets the scene	**The two scenes** deal with two key moments in the play. The first brings together Benedick and Beatrice, whilst the second shows us Benedick dealing with the consequences of the trick played on him by Claudio and Don Pedro.
First point about Benedick	**The main impression we get** of Benedick in Act 1 Scene 1 is of a vain, independent bachelor, who readily trades insults with Beatrice:
Supporting quotation	'What, my dear Lady Disdain! Are you yet living?'
Explanation and development	In other words, Benedick delights in trading jokes, but especially so with Beatrice — a pleasure that will turn swiftly to love and affection later in the play. Even here, he argues that Beatrice 'exceeds' Hero in beauty. The impression given is of someone unaware that he himself is in love.
Contrary argument, supported with evidence	But, on the surface, he sticks to his principle to 'live a bachelor' and makes fun of Claudio's romantic feelings for Hero.
Connectives of time link to next points	So, **firstly** we have seen Benedick battle with Beatrice, **then** partly reveal his attraction for her, despite her insults towards him. **Later** in the scene we see Benedick claim that nothing will make him fall in love and we get the impression he continues to be arrogant and vain. It is this that makes Don Pedro determined to make a fool of him. As Don Pedro says, 'I shall see thee, ere I die, look pale with love...'
Supporting quotation	Typically, Benedick answers that many things will make him change and grow pale — but never love. How that will change in later scenes!

TIP

When the question asks about 'impressions of a character' **use the word 'impression' in your answer**.

For example, 'the main impression we get is...'

This will help you to **stick to the point**. Also, it is likely that these impressions will be **adjectives**:

He is *vain, independent, witty* etc.

This example deals with the **second** part of the answer, which contains:

- **Act 2 Scene 3** (the end section)
- **The conclusion**.

*do **brilliantly** !*

This paragraph shows how Benedick is different in this scene

> The concluding part of **Act 2 Scene 3** presents Benedick in quite a different light. **In contrast to Act 1 Scene 1** he is **now** no longer sure of himself. The impression we get is of someone who is able now to **show love**.

Supporting quotation

> He says, he will be 'horribly in love' which suggests it's still a bit of an act. He even says he will be a 'villain' if he does not show 'pity of her', meaning Beatrice — as if he is doing her a favour! Perhaps some of his old arrogance, as seen earlier, is still there. He can't quite see the truth about his feelings, though he is much more humble than before.

This point links back to previous scene

More quotations

> However, whereas he previously might have reacted with a spiteful and cutting remark to Beatrice when she speaks to him — he now chooses to see a **'double meaning'** in her comments — and is therefore choosing to love her.

Comparison drawn

> This is very important because he now wants to create the impression that he is capable of love, **whereas** earlier he had wanted to present the opposite view — that he was incapable of loving or marrying.

Summing up connective

Conclusion brings together the earlier points

> **On the whole**, the impression given of Benedick in **these two scenes** is of someone who firstly hides what he feels under a veil of quick wit and vanity. But as the second scene shows, when the opportunity for real love is presented, he grabs it with both hands, regardless of the jokes and comments it will bring.

QUICK CHECK

Here is a typical question:

> Act 1 Scene 1
> Act 5 Scene 4
>
> **How does Shakespeare explore the idea of different types of love in these two scenes?**

- Write the **opening paragraph** for this essay. Give a *very brief* summary of what happens (no more than 40 words).
- Write the **second paragraph**, dealing with Act 1 Scene 1. Make **one point** about love in this scene, and **support it with a quotation**. Use **connectives** to link what you say.

6 What makes a top answer

However well you know the play, it is vital you understand what it takes to get **really high marks** in the Test. There are specific features that examiners are looking for and if you do not meet the criteria, you won't get the level. So, a good way to get top marks is to **know exactly what they are looking for**.

Every time I get the same level! What can I do to move up?

Features of Test levels

The following are guidelines only but they should give you a good idea of the sorts of things Test markers are looking for.

Lower level answers: level 4

- The student tends to **re-tell the plot** or events rather than comment.
- There are **irrelevant comments or information** (nothing to do with the question).
- The ideas are **poorly-expressed** using lazy or informal language.
- **Quotations** (if included) are copied out **without any real link** to the comments.
- Ideas **lack detail** and are undeveloped.
- One scene is sometimes **ignored**.

Medium level answers: level 5 to low level 6

- There is **more comment and analysis** of the scenes but **not always well-expressed**.
- There is some **development of ideas**, but it only goes so far.
- There is **an attempt to link evidence** (like quotations) **to points** made but it is done rather clumsily.
- **Some detail** on specific points is included; others are still dealt with rather too simply.

Higher level answers: high level 6 to level 7

do brilliantly!

- There is **wide comment and analysis** covering a range of ideas.
- Ideas are **fully developed**.
- There are suggestions of **other possibilities**, rather than one answer only.
- There is a clear **focus on details** and their relevance to the question.
- The points made show **insight** (looking beyond the obvious).
- **Evidence** is skilfully **woven into the writing**.

TIP

No marker expects you to write down every single thing you know about a scene. It is far better to **explore two or three key points in detail with relevant quotations**, than write down everything without any detailed comment or insight.

Here a student has written about the impressions we get of Claudio in
Act 4 Scene 1 when he rejects Hero and accuses her of being unfaithful.
This is just part of the answer.

Good start mentioning the impressions we get of Claudio, but rather poorly-expressed: ('*really nasty*', '*in this bit*').

Tries to support the point with a quotation but not really the best choice. Better to use the one where he calls Hero a '*rotten orange*'.

Explanation here, but more needed.

Tries to link a comment on Claudio's words later but no real reason is given for doing this. The point could do with evidence and explanation.

The last part seems to be more about telling us what happened. Where is the comment? Does this show he is ready to take control?

> Claudio seems **really nasty** here **in this bit** because he says lots of horrible things about Hero that aren't true and when he says he doesn't want to marry her.
>
> '**There, Leonato, take her back again...**'
>
> **Claudio is saying** that Hero's father can take her back — he doesn't want her, which isn't a nice thing to say to someone when you are supposed to be marrying their daughter!
>
> **And what** Leonato says later shows that what Claudio says isn't even that bad. Besides, why does Claudio do this now? Why did he have to shame her in public?
>
> **Then Claudio** asks Hero lots of questions about her behaviour **and what** she was doing last night, **and** Hero says she wasn't doing anything. **Then she** faints and everyone thinks she's dead at first. Claudio leaves with Don Pedro.

Marker's comment

This response:
- does attempt to talk about the impressions we get of Claudio, but does so rather clumsily
- has too much re-telling of events — Hero's fainting, Claudio rejecting Hero, Claudio questioning Hero. There is not enough explanation about what this tells us about Claudio.
- refers to Claudio's treatment of Hero as 'really nasty' but does not develop the point. Is 'nasty' the right word choice? This does not give the reader the sense of Claudio's feeling of dishonour and shame.
- uses a supporting quotation but one that does not especially help us to understand Claudio — and it is put in the answer rather suddenly.
- has a good point about Leonato speaking equally strongly about Hero, but this is undeveloped.

This is a just about a **level 5**, but only just.

Moving this response up a level

do brilliantly!

Now look at part of the same answer, rewritten to include the things the marker has indicated need to be improved or altered. The new text is in orange.

The word 'impression' is used from the start to make sure the answer is relevant.

Ideas are linked together using simple link phrases, such as 'for example'.

The chosen quotation is relevant as it shows the strength and depth of Claudio's feelings.

This is then explained to the reader.

Connective 'however' links us to the new impression. There is also more detail than before.

'Yet' signals a further idea, which is supported by the quotation by Leonato about his daughter.

'So' is used to introduce a summing up of the points made so far.

The impression given of Claudio ~~seems really nasty~~ here in this ~~bit~~ scene is of someone who is vengeful and spiteful. For example, when he rejects Hero and gives her back to her father. ~~because he says lots of horrible things about Hero that aren't true and when he says he doesn't want to marry her.~~ Claudio tells him:

'There, Leonato, take her back again,
Give not this rotten orange to your friend.'

Claudio is taking the ultimate revenge in this way; the revenge of the wronged fiancé who chooses a very public humiliation. However, this says much more about Claudio and his lack of judgement than it does about Hero's honour.
Yet ~~And~~ what Leonato says later shows that ~~what~~ Claudio's language is not out of place. Leonato feels equally dishonoured, possibly more so, and he doesn't have the excuse of only partly knowing Hero. He even says he wishes he'd had an adopted 'beggar's issue' rather than had Hero as a daughter. The truth is that neither man can be excused their words, whatever the provocation. Both show lack of trust and understanding of this woman whom they both love. ~~says isn't even that bad. Besides why does Claudio do this now? Why did he have to shame her in public?~~
So, we are given, in Claudio, the impression of a man driven to the worst type of revenge by the shame he feels, and the dishonour he has suffered. His final words in the scene sum up how little he can distinguish between good and bad, as he says, 'Most foul, most fair, farewell' to Hero as he leaves.

Marker's comment

I see the difference – detail, evidence, explanation, style!

This response now:
- links the points made effectively
- develops ideas more fully
- uses relevant quotations and explains what they mean
- keeps the focus on the question – the impressions we get of Claudio
- reads fluently, with an appropriate style and tone (nothing too chatty or informal).

Overall level: **(high) level 6/borderline level 7**, on the evidence of this section.

Gaining the highest level

In order to get the highest marks possible, however, your answer needs to have **something special**. You need to mix two very important things:

- **insight** – looking beyond the obvious and really seeing into the heart of the play and its characters.
- **imaginative and detailed expression of your ideas** – you need to write your ideas down in a way that will appeal to the Test marker.

Paragraph structure

Here is one example of how one small part of the Claudio answer might be written:

What happens

The student states what happens clearly and concisely. There is no re-telling of the story.

> As Claudio rejects Hero, is he also rejecting the innocent life of the carefree young man. He is learning that the world can be cruel and that what is outwardly decent might be 'rotten'.
>
> He understands in what way 'authority and show of truth/Can cunning sin cover itself...'
>
> Yet, what he fails to see — and what makes his 'growing up' incomplete, is that he has seen sin in the wrong place. Rather than recognise it in Don John he sees it in the last imaginable place — Hero.
>
> He is deaf to Hero's words of innocence, hearing only what he now wants to hear. He almost enjoys taking the moral high ground.

Insight/suggestion

This insight into Claudio's journey comes from the student knowing the play very well — from knowing that Claudio will suffer even more later.

Quotation

Note how well the quotation is *woven into* the point made – the expression is excellent.

Explanation and development

Finally, the points are linked to new information.

QUICK CHECK

Improve the extract below from a level 5/6 answer.

You will need to **express** the ideas better; and **show insight** into **why** Don Pedro might say what he says in this scene (Act 4 Scene 1). Use an actual quotation.

> When Don Pedro is asked why he's not saying anything he's dead cross because he's really upset by what has happened. After all, he saw Hero being unfaithful so he knows about it. And he's the Prince after all, isn't he?

This section contains:

- **two practice questions** on the set scenes for *Much Ado About Nothing* (see pages 73 and 84)
- a mark scheme for you to assess your own work and get a good idea of the **level requirements** (see pages 78 and 89)
- **sample answers** at different levels (see pages 79–83 and 90–94) with comments to help you improve your level.

Before turning to the Test questions, **read the information on this page carefully**.

Some important points

The set scenes from *Much Ado About Nothing* for the 2005 Shakespeare Paper are as follows:

> **Act 1 Scene 1 (lines 119–215):**
> *'Benedick, didst thou note the daughter of Signor Leonato?'*
> to
> *'...examine your conscience: and so I leave you.'*
> and
>
> **Act 2 Scene 3 (lines 81 to the end of the scene):**
> *'Come hither, Leonato, what was it you told me of today,'*
> to
> *'if I do not love her I am a Jew, I will go get her picture'*

> Yes, **read** the instructions first... That way I am sure I will know what to do!

- You will **not be given all** of each of these scenes in the actual Test.
- You will be given **one question about shorter extracts** from **the two scenes**.

The practice questions that follow are just two **possible** questions that could be asked, so do not think that you can learn the answers word for word for the Test or you will get a nasty shock! Therefore, it is important you revise all the set scenes mentioned above so that you don't get caught out.

Now **read question 1** and the extracts from the set scenes (on pages 74–77). Read the question carefully and remember to **plan your answer before you start to write**.

It is a good idea to **time yourself** when you revise like this – **you will only have 45 minutes in the Test!**

Remember

- Respond to the **question that has been set**, using the **key words from the question**.
- Write **clearly** using **whole sentences** and **paragraphs**.
- **Support** your points with **evidence** and **quotations**.
- **Link your ideas together** using **connectives**.
- **Check your writing** to see it is **clear** and **makes sense**.

QUESTION 1

You should spend about 45 minutes on this question.

Much Ado About Nothing

Act 1 Scene 1, lines 131 to 199
Act 2 Scene 3, lines 181 to the end of the scene

What impressions might an audience get of Benedick from the different ways he speaks and behaves in these two extracts?

Much Ado About Nothing

Act 1 Scene 1, lines 131 to 199

> In this extract, Claudio has asked Benedick for his opinion of Hero, who he has fallen in love with.

CLAUDIO	Thou thinkest I am in sport. I pray thee, tell me truly how thou lik'st her?
BENEDICK	Would you buy her, that you enquire after her?
CLAUDIO	Can the world buy such a jewel?
BENEDICK	Yea, and a case to put it into. But speak you this with a sad brow? Or do you play the flouting Jack, to tell us Cupid is a good hare-finder, and Vulcan a rare carpenter? Come, in what key shall a man take you, to go in the song?
CLAUDIO	In mine eye, she is the sweetest lady that ever I looked on.
BENEDICK	I can see yet without spectacles, and I see no such matter. There's her cousin, and she were not possessed with a fury, exceeds her as much in beauty as the first of May doth the last of December. But I hope you have no intent to turn husband, have you?
CLAUDIO	I would scarce trust myself, though I had sworn the contrary, if Hero would be my wife.
BENEDICK	Is't come to this? In faith, hath not the world one man, but he will wear his cap with suspicion? Shall I never see a bachelor of three score again? Go to, i'faith, and thou wilt needs thrust thy neck into a yoke, wear the print of it, and sigh away Sundays. Look, Don Pedro is returned to seek you.

Enter DON PEDRO

DON PEDRO	What secret hath held you here, that you followed not to Leonato's?
BENEDICK	I would your grace would constrain me to tell.
DON PEDRO	I charge thee on thy allegiance.
BENEDICK	You hear, Count Claudio, I can be secret as a dumb man – I would have you think so. But on my allegiance (mark you this, on my allegiance) he is in love. With who? Now that is your grace's part: mark how short his answer is. With Hero, Leonato's short daughter.

Line numbers: 135, 140, 145, 150

CLAUDIO	If this were so, so were it uttered.	
BENEDICK	Like the old tale, my lord: 'It is not so, nor 'twas not so, but indeed, God forbid it should be so.'	160
CLAUDIO	If my passion change not shortly, God forbid it should be otherwise.	
DON PEDRO	Amen, if you love her, for the lady is very well worthy.	
CLAUDIO	You speak this to fetch me in, my lord.	165
DON PEDRO	By my troth, I speak my thought.	
CLAUDIO	And in faith, my lord, I spoke mine.	
BENEDICK	And by my two faiths and troths, my lord, I spoke mine.	
CLAUDIO	That I love her, I feel.	
DON PEDRO	That she is worthy, I know.	170
BENEDICK	That I neither feel how she should be loved, nor know how she should be worthy, is the opinion that fire cannot melt out of me: I will die in it at the stake.	
DON PEDRO	Thou wast ever an obstinate heretic in the despite of beauty.	
CLAUDIO	And never could maintain his part, but in the force of his will.	175
BENEDICK	That a woman conceived me, I thank her: that she brought me up, I likewise give her most humble thanks: but that I will have a recheat winded in my forehead, or hang my bugle in an invisible baldrick, all women shall pardon me. Because I will not do them the wrong to mistrust any, I will do myself the right to trust none: and the fine is (for the which I may go the finer) I will live a bachelor.	180
DON PEDRO	I shall see thee, ere I die, look pale with love.	
BENEDICK	With anger, with sickness, or with hunger, my lord, not with love: prove that ever I lose more blood with love than I will get again with drinking, pick out mine eyes with a ballad-maker's pen, and hang me up at the door of a brothel house for the sign of blind Cupid.	185

1

| DON PEDRO | Well, if ever thou dost fall from this faith, thou wilt prove a notable argument. | 190 |

| BENEDICK | If I do, hang me in a bottle like a cat, and shoot at me, and he that hits me, let him be clapped on the shoulder, and called Adam. | |

| DON PEDRO | Well, as time shall try: 'In time the savage bull doth bear the yoke.' | |

| BENEDICK | The savage bull may, but if ever the sensible Benedick bear it, pluck off the bull's horns, and set them in my forehead, and let me be vilely painted, and in such great letters as they write, 'Here is good horse to hire', let them signify under my sign, 'Here you may see Benedick the married man.' | 195 |

Act 2 Scene 3 (lines 181 to the end of the scene)

In this extract, Benedick has just overheard Leonato, Don Pedro and Claudio speaking about Beatrice saying that she loves him (Benedick).

| BENEDICK | This can be no trick, the conference was sadly borne, they have the truth of this from Hero, they seem to pity the lady: it seems her affections have their full bent: love me? Why, it must be requited: I hear how I am censured, they say I will bear myself proudly, if I perceive the love come from her: they say too, that she will rather die than give any sign of affection: I did never think to marry, I must not seem proud, happy are they that hear their detrac– tions, and can put them to mending: they say the lady is fair, 'tis a truth, I can bear them witness: and virtuous, 'tis so, I cannot reprove it; and wise, but for loving me: by my troth it is no addition to her wit, nor no great argument of her folly, for I will be horribly in love with her: I may chance have some odd quirks and remnants of wit broken on me, because I have railed so long against marriage: but doth not the appetite alter? A man loves the meat in his youth, that he cannot endure in his age. Shall quips and sentences, and these paper bullets of the brain awe a man from the career of his humour? No, the world must be peopled. When I said I would die a bachelor, I did not think I should live till I were married – here comes Beatrice: by this day, she's a fair lady, I do spy some marks of love in her. | 185

190

195

200 |

Enter BEATRICE

BEATRICE   Against my will I am sent to bid you come in to dinner.

BENEDICK   Fair Beatrice, I thank you for your pains.

BEATRICE   I took no more pains for those thanks, than you took pains to
thank me, if it had been painful, I would not have come.

BENEDICK   You take pleasure then in the message?   205

BEATRICE   Yea, just so much as you may take upon a knife's point, and
choke a daw withal: you have no stomach, signor, fare you well.

Exeunt

BENEDICK   Ha, against my will I am sent to bid you come in to dinner:
there's a double meaning in that: I took no more pains for those
thanks than you take pains to thank me: that's as much as to say, any
pains that I take for you is as easy as thanks: if I do not take pity of
her I am a villain, if I do not love her I am a Jew, I will go get her
picture.

Exeunt

1

Level indicators for question 1

Now it is time to **check the level** of your own response to question 1 (see page 73) and to see how you may be able to improve your answer.

At the beginning of this section (page 72), you were advised to make sure that you **answer** the question set, **support** your points with **evidence** from the text and lastly that you **check your writing** to see that it **makes sense**.

Use the table below to assess the level of your work. Look at the indicators against each level and decide where your answer best fits.

There are also sample answers provided (see pages 79–83). Each sample answer is at a different level. You will probably find it useful to compare these with your own answer to get the best idea of your level.

Level	Indicators
4	• A few simple ideas about how Benedick changes between the two scenes. Perhaps saying that Benedick doesn't think much of women to start with but is ready to do anything for Beatrice in the second scene. • Some explanation of the dialogue, supported by some quotations. These are not always relevant, and are rather clumsily inserted into the answer. • Some reference to the fact that in the second extract Benedick is going back on what he had previously said. • More reference to the story/plot than insight into Benedick's character. • Poor style means that ideas seem un-linked and not thought through.
5	• Greater understanding of the impressions we get of Benedick, perhaps focusing on how he enjoys making fun of Claudio's feelings for Hero, and how his mocking might come across as 'arrogant'. Candidate also comments that Benedick seems fairly certain that he will not fall for someone. • Demonstrates some understanding that the audience is not completely convinced by Benedick's views about women. For all Benedick claims not to want a woman, he seem to like talking about them! • Student only quotes the more obvious comments, e.g. *'I will live a bachelor'*. Not much enquiry into the sort of change we see in the second scene – does he seem ridiculous? Does he seem sad? • Accurate use of paragraphs and reasonably helpful style and structure, but the points are not very fluent or well-linked.
6	• Closer and more detailed examination of the language, and what this tells us about Benedick. Perhaps there is reference to the way his comments about Hero are like the punch lines of jokes. • A clearer focus on the change in Benedick – how his words *'Love me?'* in the second scene could come across almost sadly – as if he believed he would never be truly loved. • Some understanding of the way, even now, Benedick is too proud to admit he is wrong and is still explaining his earlier words to himself *('When I said I would die a bachelor, I did not think I should live till I were married...')* • A much greater focus on language. Student comments on individual words and phrases related to Benedick and what they tell us about him. • Answer is well-written in clear, well-linked paragraphs. Ideas are fluently expressed.
7	• Clear development of all points made, with focused analysis of Benedick's behaviour and language. • Comments that we initially see Benedick as a lively joker, who appears to know all about women, someone who is witty and rather vain. Student discusses how Benedick later changes to show signs of insecurity and self-doubt. • Answer may suggest that Benedick, especially in the second extract, could be seen as shocked, unsure and even lonely. Comments that Benedick also appears rather foolish in this scene (he himself seems to be aware of this – *'I may chance have some odd quirks and remnants of wit broken on me...'*). Student does not fail to note that equally we could admire him for being ready to face ridicule for love. • Quotations are wide and varied, and there is good knowledge of the play as a whole and the function played by these specific scenes within it. • Answer shows insight and is fully developed with ideas explored in a fluent and coherent way. • Answer is individual, with a clear style and the student shows flair in both their analysis and use of language.

Sample answers to question 1

Student A

The comments to these sample answers are colour-coded to help you identify the weak or strong areas. When a box is **green** it means that the student has done something well, **amber** indicates that some **improvement is needed**, and **red** means that the student needs to look again and maybe go back to the drawing-board!

Useful, relevant comment, although style is too informal.

Another quotation but it is inappropriate.

No full stop!

New paragraph but the main focus seems to be re-telling the story and the style is very sloppy and informal.

Reference to effect created for the audience.

Good use of quotation.

Reasonable attempt to sum up Benedick's change but not very detailed.

> Benedick is very different to the audience in these two scenes cos in the first, Act 1 Scene 1, he seems quite full of himself and says 'I will live a bachelor' which is a single man who lives on his own and isn't tied down or anything. This is because his best friend Claudio fancies this girl called Hero who is the daughter of Leonato. Claudio asks for Benedick's advice which is funny cos Benedick doesn't really like women much.
>   'That a women conceived me I thank her' I think that he comes across as a bit snobbish or something when he says that
>   Later he is in Act 2 Scene 3 and he listened to what the others like Claudio and Pedro said. They wanted him to fall in love with Beatrice which they thought would be well funny because Beatrice and Benedick hate each other. This can be seen earlier when they are insulting each other.
>   Anyway back to the story. In this bit Benedick is hiding and hears them say that Beatrice loves him which he can't believe. He must be completely shocked by this I think and he would act shocked. But the main thing is that he changes how he speaks and starts saying how he will love Beatrice then when she comes out he doesn't argue much with her just does what she says.
>   He says 'Fair Beatrice' which before he would have been taking the mickey and she probably thinks he is this time.
>   So he is completely different in the second scene because he has become all nice and loving and isn't going to insult her now because he was tricked by the others.

This is not a word in English! Slang!

Quotation supports the point made, although is explained clumsily.

Some attempt at an explanation of the quotation, although informal style.

This sentence is too long and should not start with 'but'. Good comment on Benedick' change, although a quote to illustrate would improve the answer.

Informal style. Reconsider use of language.

Marker's summary

- This response shows some awareness of the more obvious changes in Benedick from one scene to the other, but the ideas are rather undeveloped and quotations are used without much thought.
- This would gain a **mid level 4** mark.

Student B

In the first scene Benedick gives the impression of someone who thinks he is quite funny and is always making jokes. We can even remember before this bit begins that he has had lots of conversations and insults with Beatrice, so we know he likes a joke. So now when he is asked what Hero is like he says, 'I can see without spectacles'. This is a sort of joke saying he doesn't need help to look at women and what they're like.

Starts by using the word from the title to make a relevant point.

Quotation supports the point made, though it is not really a 'joke'.

But he also is quite arrogant because he says how women and love aren't that important to him.

Don Pedro: I shall see thee, ere I die, look pale with love.

Benedick: With anger, with sickness, or with hunger, my lord, not with love...

So he even argues with his boss Don Pedro saying that nothing will make him fall in love.

New point made about his character, supported by a longer quotation although there is little detail here.

Some attempt at an explanation of the quotation.

But in Act 2 Scene 3 he listens secretly to what Claudio and Pedro say and this changes how he speaks. Now he is all worried about himself and his behaviour.

'I hear how I am censured, they say I will bear myself proudly...'

New paragraph for new points.

'But' is not the best choice of connective.

This makes him seem not quite so vain. It can't be very nice hearing all those things said about you. So now he seems a different person — the opposite of before. Before he made fun of marriage and love. Now he is saying that, 'I will be horribly in love with her,' which means he will really show her what love is. This fits a bit with his character as even in love he has to be the best.

Good comment on Benedick's change, and some development of the point (although not that detailed or fluently expressed).

Attempt to sum up Benedick's change, although not very detailed.

But the main point is that he is changing and is trying to be a different person. It's like he's sort of guilty about how he behaved before.

'I must not seem proud, happy are they that hear their detrac-tions, and can put them to mending...'

He is saying that when people criticise you, you must learn from it. And this means when Beatrice appears he behaves in a different way. This time he says 'Fair Beatrice' and he means it.

In the end the impression the audience gets of Benedick is someone who has found something more important than making jokes and saying how great he is.

Before he was a bit of a clown but this shows that he really wants to be loved so that when Beatrice says she takes pleasure in seeing him, like someone takes pleasure killing a bird, he thinks she is talking with a two meanings and that it proves she loves him.

Point is supported by relevant quotation and further explanation.

Tries to draw conclusions about Benedick. Good but a bit limited.

Refers back to earlier scene.

Could do with a quotation here to support the point.

Marker's summary

- This response shows a deeper awareness of the different impressions an audience is likely to get about Benedick from one scene to the other.

- However, some of the earlier points could be developed and there is not enough about Benedick's behaviour and language in the first extract. The comments on the second are much better and more developed, and there is a useful conclusion.

- Quotations are generally well-chosen but are sometimes clumsily placed in the text, making the points made seem rather plodding.

- This response would gain a **level 5**.

Student C

Good introduction to the point, using keyword from the title and mentioning the audience.

Adjectives are used to describe the impressions he gives.

New paragraph for next point.

Further point and more development of ideas, although is this the very best choice of language?

Fresh thinking offered but unsupported by evidence. How was he 'before'?

Benedick gives **quite different impressions to the audience in the two scenes,** although at the core he perhaps keeps certain elements of his character.

In the first scene, an important point is that we see Benedick with other people: he is **showing-off,** and not surprisingly he comes across as rather **arrogant** and **vain.** He 'thanks' his mother for giving birth to him and bringing him up, but asks that **'all women' excuse him from being tied down as a** husband.

Another key impression the audience get of Benedick is as a joker, anxious to display his wit and entertain others. When Claudio and Don Pedro are discussing Hero's virtues, Benedick adds his comments, like punch-lines.

Don Pedro: **By my troth, I speak my thought.**
Claudio: And in faith, my lord, I spoke mine.
Benedick: And by my two faiths and troths, my lord, I spoke mine.

It would perhaps be **too strong to say that Benedick is a woman-hater** — after all most (except Beatrice) seem to put up with his company, but we certainly get the impression that he doesn't want to be ruled or controlled by them. As he says :
'Shall I never see a bachelor of three score again?' and calls marriage **'a yoke'** (a harness to control horses!).

He adds later that many things will make him sigh ('anger', 'sickness' and 'hunger') but not love. He is convinced he will never be in harness to women.

Yet, perhaps this is all an act? After all, he is performing for Don Pedro and Claudio. Perhaps they expect him to act like that — to be the clown? **This fits with how he has been before.**

Behaviour is also mentioned, not just language.

Relevant quotation and paraphrasing support points.

Relevant quotations used to develop points.

Relevant short and long quotations used to develop points, plus explanation.

New scene introduced by new paragraph, fluently linked.

Of course, at the end of Act 2 Scene 3, a different Benedick emerges. He is on his own and so what we hear him say can be taken to be the truth. He is no longer showing-off. Now, the impression the audience gets, is of a man who is shocked by what he hears. He rambles, speaking in long sentences, and some of his thoughts seem unconnected:

'I did never think to marry, I must not seem too proud, happy are they that hear their detractions, and can put them to mending...'

Contrasts with earlier scene and comments.

Explanation followed by relevant quotation.

Quotation backs up new explanation.

It is as if Benedick has suddenly woken up — and what he has heard seems to make him twist around what he has said earlier:

'When I said I would die a bachelor, I did not think I should live till I were married...'

Develops explanation – shows insight.

He confirms his 'change of heart' by adding later in the same speech:

'...doth not the appetite (for marriage) alter?'

Short sentence excellent for showing viewpoint.

This is all nonsense of course. He is only saying these things now, to prove to himself that what he is doing is justified. You could get the impression he's a bit of a hypocrite. Or that he should be pitied — perhaps he really didn't think anyone would love him?

This idea could be developed with suitable quotation.

No real conclusion or summing up.

Anyway, our final impression of him is someone who is desperate for love, and who is delighted when Beatrice appears to call him in for dinner.

Ends a bit weakly. Where is the evidence – quotation?

Marker's summary

- This is a detailed, coherent response that is well-structured and well-argued. The quotations chosen are all relevant, and are carefully woven into the points the student is making.
- The question is fully answered and the student also shows insight, going beyond the obvious to provide more detailed explanations.
- The conclusion is rather weak, and one or two points need further evidence, but all in all this is a strong answer.
- It would gain a **level 7**.

You should spend about 45 minutes on this question.

Much Ado About Nothing

Act 1 Scene 1, lines 119 to 188
Act 2 Scene 3, lines 166 to 200

**What different ideas about women are
explored by Shakespeare in these two extracts?**

Much Ado About Nothing

Act 1 Scene 1, lines 119 to 188

> **In this extract, Claudio asks Benedick for his opinion of Hero, whom he has fallen in love with.**

CLAUDIO	Benedick, didst thou note the daughter of Signor Leonato?	
BENEDICK	I noted her not, but I looked on her.	120
CLAUDIO	Is she a modest young lady?	
BENEDICK	Do you question me as an honest man should do, for my simple true judgement? Or would you have me speak after my custom, as being a professed tyrant to their sex?	
CLAUDIO	No, I pray thee speak in sober judgement.	125
BENEDICK	Why i'faith, methinks she's too low for a high praise, too brown for a fair praise, and too little for a great praise. Only this commendation I can afford her, that were she other than she is, she were unhandsome, and being no other, but as she is – I do not like her.	130
CLAUDIO	Thou thinkest I am in sport. I pray thee, tell me truly how thou lik'st her?	
BENEDICK	Would you buy her, that you enquire after her?	
CLAUDIO	Can the world buy such a jewel?	
BENEDICK	Yea, and a case to put it into. But speak you this with a sad brow? Or do you play the flouting Jack, to tell us Cupid is a good hare-finder, and Vulcan a rare carpenter? Come, in what key shall a man take you, to go in the song?	135
CLAUDIO	In mine eye, she is the sweetest lady that ever I looked on.	
BENEDICK	I can see yet without spectacles, and I see no such matter. There's her cousin, and she were not possessed with a fury, exceeds her as much in beauty as the first of May doth the last of December. But I hope you have no intent to turn husband, have you?	140
CLAUDIO	I would scarce trust myself, though I had sworn the contrary, if Hero would be my wife.	145

2

BENEDICK	Is't come to this? In faith, hath not the world one man, but he will wear his cap with suspicion? Shall I never see a bachelor of three score again? Go to, i'faith, and thou wilt needs thrust thy neck into a yoke, wear the print of it, and sigh away Sundays. Look, Don Pedro is returned to seek you.

150

Enter DON PEDRO

DON PEDRO	What secret hath held you here, that you followed not to Leonato's?
BENEDICK	I would your grace would constrain me to tell.
DON PEDRO	I charge thee on thy allegiance.
BENEDICK	You hear, Count Claudio, I can be secret as a dumb man; I would have you think so. But on my allegiance (mark you this, on my allegiance) he is in love. With who? Now that is your grace's part: mark how short his answer is. With Hero, Leonato's short daughter.
CLAUDIO	If this were so, so were it uttered.
BENEDICK	Like the old tale, my lord: 'It is not so, nor 'twas not so, but indeed, God forbid it should be so.'
CLAUDIO	If my passion change not shortly, God forbid it should be otherwise.
DON PEDRO	Amen, if you love her, for the lady is very well worthy.
CLAUDIO	You speak this to fetch me in, my lord.
DON PEDRO	By my troth, I speak my thought.
CLAUDIO	And in faith, my lord, I spoke mine.
BENEDICK	And by my two faiths and troths, my lord, I spoke mine.
CLAUDIO	That I love her, I feel.
DON PEDRO	That she is worthy, I know.
BENEDICK	That I neither feel how she should be loved nor know how she should be worthy, is the opinion that fire cannot melt out of me: I will die in it at the stake.

155

160

165

170

DON PEDRO	Thou wast ever an obstinate heretic in the despite of beauty.	
CLAUDIO	And never could maintain his part, but in the force of his will.	175
BENEDICK	That a woman conceived me, I thank her: that she brought me up, I likewise give her most humble thanks: but that I will have a recheat winded in my forehead, or hang my bugle in an invisible baldrick, all women shall pardon me. Because I will not do them the wrong to mistrust any, I will do myself the right to trust none: and the fine is (for the which I may go the finer) I will live a bachelor.	180
DON PEDRO	I shall see thee, ere I die, look pale with love.	
BENEDICK	With anger, with sickness, or with hunger, my lord, not with love: prove that ever I lose more blood with love than I will get again with drinking, pick out mine eyes with a ballad-maker's pen, and hang me up at the door of a brothel house for the sign of blind Cupid.	185

Act 2 Scene 3, lines 166 to 200

> **In this extract, Benedick is listening to Leonato, Don Pedro and Claudio who are talking about Beatrice's love for him (Benedick).**

DON PEDRO	…well, I am sorry for your niece: shall we go seek Benedick, and tell him of her love?	
CLAUDIO	Never tell him, my lord, let her wear it out with good counsel.	
LEONATO	Nay that's impossible, she may wear her heart out first.	
DON PEDRO	Well, we will hear further of it by your daughter, let it cool the while: I love Benedick well, and I could wish he would modestly examine himself, to see how much he is unworthy so good a lady.	170
LEONATO	My lord, will you walk? Dinner is ready.	
CLAUDIO	If he do not dote on her upon this, I will never trust my expectation.	175

DON PEDRO	Let there be the same net spread for her, and that must your daughter and her gentlewoman carry: the sport will be, when they hold one an opinion of another's dotage, and no such matter: that's the scene that I would see, which will be merely a dumb show: let us send her to call him in to dinner. 180

Exeunt all but Benedick

BENEDICK	This can be no trick, the conference was sadly borne, they have the truth of this from Hero, they seem to pity to lady: it seems her affections have their full bent: love me? Why, it must be requited: I hear how I am censured, they say I will bear myself proudly, if I perceive the love come from her: they say too, that she 185 will rather die than give any sign of affection: I did never think to marry, I must not seem proud, happy are they that hear their detrac– tions, and can put them to mending: they say the lady is fair, 'tis a truth, I can bear them witness: and virtuous, 'tis so, I cannot reprove it: and wise, but for loving me: by my troth it is no addition to her 190 wit, nor no great argument of her folly, for I will be horribly in love with her: I may chance have some odd quirks and remnants of wit broken on me, because I have railed so long against marriage: but doth not the appetite alter? A man loves the meat in his youth, that he cannot endure in his age. Shall quips and sentences, and these 195 paper bullets of the brain awe a man from the career of his humour? No, the world must be peopled. When I said I would die a bachelor, I did not think I should live till I were married – here comes Beatrice: by this day, she's a fair lady, I do spy some marks of love in 200 her.

Level indicators for question 2

Now it is time to **check the level** of your own response to question 2 (see page 84) and to see how you may be able to improve your answer.

There are also sample answers provided (see pages 90–94). Each sample answer is at a different level. You will probably find it useful to compare these with your own answer to get the best idea of your level.

Level	Indicators
4	<ul><li>Some simple ideas about how women are described but there is too much about the characters themselves and not enough about how Shakespeare's ideas are explored *through* them.</li><li>Some explanation of what is said, supported by some quotations, but these are not always relevant, and are rather clumsily inserted into the answer.</li><li>No attempt to draw ideas together.</li><li>Poor style makes ideas seem un-linked and not thought through.</li></ul>
5	<ul><li>Greater understanding of the points Shakespeare is making about women, but still a tendency to focus on the characters and not *explain what this tells us*.</li><li>Some basic quotations and references used but still rather poorly inserted into the response.</li><li>The response does not delve in any depth into the views and ideas Shakespeare is exploring.</li><li>Accurate and reasonably helpful style and structure, but not very fluent or well linked.</li></ul>
6	<ul><li>Closer and more detailed examination of the language and what it tells us about Shakespeare's views. There is comment on the fact that the men enjoy talking and making fun of relationships and that Benedick is pretty arrogant about women and what they mean to men.</li><li>Some understanding of the role of women in the play as objects of beauty and modesty, but little comment on who is powerful, and who pulls the strings (in Shakespeare's day this was men) nor about who is actually smarter (Beatrice, for example).</li><li>A much greater focus on language: the individual words and phrases related to the theme are explored and there is development and comment on them.</li><li>Answer is well-written in clear, well-linked paragraphs. Ideas are fluently expressed.</li></ul>
7	<ul><li>Clear development of all points made with focused analysis on the language of the two scenes and what this tells us about Shakespeare's thoughts on women in the play.</li><li>There may be comment on the role of women in Shakespeare's day and how the views of the characters reflect this: women as commodities, objects of beauty and innocence, but not necessarily equal partners.</li><li>Good answers may suggest that Benedick is used by Shakespeare as a way of exploring how men relate to women. He demonstrates how relationships can be improved when one is not just looking for love, but also someone who is equal in other ways.</li><li>Quotations are wide and varied, and there is good knowledge of the play as a whole and these scenes' part in it.</li><li>Answer shows insight and is fully developed with ideas explored in a fluent and coherent way.</li><li>Answer is individual, with a clear style and the student shows flair in both their analysis and use of language.</li></ul>

QUESTION 2

2

Sample answers to Question 2

Student A

As with question 1, when a box is **green** it means that the student has done something well, **amber** indicates that some **improvement is needed**, and **red** means that the student needs to look again and maybe go back to the drawing-board!

Starts with a clear point of view, although style is too chatty.

Quotation is partly relevant, but not fully explained.

Slips into retelling the story – is this relevant?

Finally, a point is made about women and a quotation is given to support it.

Last point slips into retelling story and writing about Benedick.

I think that Shakespeare's view of women is a pretty bad one judging by this as there is lots of things said that aren't very nice. For example in the first bit they all seem to be making jokes about women especially Hero.

'She's too little for great praise' Benedick says about her which isn't very nice, seeing as his best mate is in love with her and all that. Later Benedick says that he'll never be married and this makes it seem like marriage is an awful thing. He even takes the mickey out of his own mother saying that all she was good for was to give birth to him! He's really sarcastic about it.

Then the others say that they'll make him fall in love and he'll change his views and that's what happens later.

In the other scene Benedick hears about Beatrice and how she loves him and how he has been mean to her. Now he is all lovey-dovey and suddenly he is all nice about women saying how Beatrice is pretty and a good person. He says, 'The world must be peopled' which means it is ok to marry and have kids and you need a woman for that, don't you?

So I suppose Shakespeare is saying that it's all very well making jokes about women but in the end you need them.

This is what Benedick says in any case, and that is why he is suddenly all over Beatrice when she comes to get him. Even if she still treats him like dirt!

Tries to add evidence, although clumsily expressed.

New paragraph needed here!

Further comment on women but marriage point is not explained.

Too chatty!

Still retelling the story, even if student is now trying to make a new point. The quote is relevant, but there is lots of comment on Benedick and not enough about women.

Explanation of quotation although style is too informal.

Marker's summary

- Some good points are made with some supporting evidence and quotations.
- Too often the student slips into retelling the story and goes off track.
- There is no real conclusion, and the ideas become chatty and vague in places.
- This response would gain a **low level 4**.

Student B

Direct and concise introduction sets the scene.

Immediately makes a comment about view of women, although it could be more elegantly expressed.

In 'Much Ado about Nothing' William Shakespeare's view of women changes from one scene to another.

In the first scene women are mostly seen as something to have a bit of a laugh about. Even Benedick knows he can talk about women in different ways depending on what people want him to do.

Offers little explanation of what this tells us about Shakespeare's view.

'Do you question me as an honest man should do, for my simple true judgement? Or would you have me speak after my custom, as being a professed tyrant to their sex?'

Quotation supports point made.

So Benedick is proud of being nasty to women! And he's not very nice about Hero after that. But he does kind of compliment Beatrice, saying :

'There's her cousin, and she were not possessed of a fury, exceeds her as much in beauty as the first of May doth the last of December...'

Second quotation to take point further.

Finally, some analysis of the points made about women but could do with more analysis.

The point is that they all talk about how women look, too. They have to be 'fair' and 'modest'. It's like women are not allowed to be like Beatrice, who is clever and witty. Only the men can be witty.

Also, Benedick says some pretty unpleasant things about marriage (which is also against women), saying how you end up stuck at home and 'sigh away' on Sundays.

Another new point but introduced a little abruptly with no link to what has been said before.

Good to refer not just to Benedick.

I suppose that Claudio at least seems nicer to women. He calls Hero a 'jewel' and wants to marry her and it is a shame that Benedick makes so much fun of it because it ruins Claudio's romantic comments.

QUESTION 2

2

New scene introduced – and interesting point made with quotations.

In the second scene, a different view of women comes out. First Don Pedro says that Benedick is 'unworthy' of Beatrice, who is so 'good a lady'. But we do have to remember this is said to trick Benedick. **Does Don Pedro really care about Beatrice's feelings, or does he just want to see a bit of fun and have a laugh?**

Use of question helps understanding, but the point made could be explored.

Further points and quotation and mention of Shakespeare, but more analysis needed for a top mark.

But Shakespeare does give us a different view of women when Benedick is alone. Now he seems almost guilty about what he said before and even says marriage may not be such a bad thing – 'I have railed so long against marriage: but doth not the appetite alter?'

Bad style to start paragraph with 'but'.

He even says that Beatrice is 'wise' except in loving him. So, now he seems to have a better view of women. Beatrice is 'fair' and 'virtuous' and her happiness seems important to him.

Relevant quotations, but what does this say *about women*; more depth needed.

He also talks about how he was criticised for his behaviour towards her (and women in general).

Good attempt to sum up and refer to essay task, but possibly needs further explanation and insight at the end.

Therefore I think Shakespeare is saying that if you can overcome your pride, you can find the right person – and love is more important than showing-off. **There seems more respect for women at the end of this scene** even though it is a trick that brings Benedick and Beatrice together.

Marker's summary

- This student makes a lot of relevant points and uses many appropriate quotations but the argument doesn't quite hang together.
- There is too much jumping from one point to another, and Shakespeare's views about women get a little lost from time to time. The conclusion tries to draw things together but makes comments about other things than the view of women.
- This response would be a **borderline level 5/6**.

Student C

Intro links ideas about women to Shakespeare's times.

Shakespeare's ideas about women in these two scenes probably reflect the way they were regarded in his own day. Yes, they are objects of beauty — and even in Act 1 Scene 1 we see the men finding it difficult to be serious and talk about feelings without making jokes about women.

Paragraph supports this point and adds further comment *about women*.

For example, according to Benedick, women are grudgingly thanked by him for giving birth and bringing him up, but are then seen as likely to betray husbands. (Benedick complains of not wanting horns in his forehead — a sign that your wife is unfaithful). Earlier he even talks about marriage as being like a 'yoke' (a horse's harness) giving the married man no freedom, leaving him to 'sigh away Sundays' stuck at home.

Relevant quotations used.

Paragraph takes idea and develops it further (expansion).

Suitable quotations support points.

It's natural that this comes across as women's fault, and what's worse women are also described as objects — things to be bought or sold (which is quite accurate for the arranged marriages of Shakespeare's day). We see this as Benedick says about Hero to Claudio: 'Would you buy her, that you enquire after her?' Claudio responds, 'Can the world buy such a jewel?'

However, it should be pointed out that it sounds like Claudio does respect Hero. He calls her 'the sweetest lady that ever I looked on'. And Don Pedro says she is 'well worthy'.

Alternative viewpoint touched upon although could be expanded.

Bad style to start with 'but'.

But the main impression given of women in this first scene is of young, beautiful and pure single women of good families like Hero being worshipped, but older married women (and men actually) being viewed with pity as fools.

This pararaph sums up what has been said so far and adds to it.

As Benedick says, if he is ever married and controlled like a harnessed horse, he should be placed under a 'vilely painted' sign as a warning to others. 'Here you may see Benedick the married man.'

QUESTION 2

Contrast drawn between the two scenes.

Of course, these views seem a world away by the time Act 2 Scene 3 has ended. Benedick has shown, when speaking on his own, how much the love of a woman — an equal partner, like Beatrice, means to him. He even questions her wisdom in loving him, saying she is 'wise, but for loving me...'

Well-used supporting quotation.

He now has a different view of women's worth. Whereas he thanked his mother rather sarcastically for bringing him into the world, he now uses this as an argument for showing love to Beatrice:

'The world must be peopled..'

Yes, but what is *Shakespeare* saying here?

Further development and quotation but some lack of explanation.

Of course, such things as Beatrice being a 'fair lady' (pretty) and 'virtuous' (i.e. decent) are still important, but Benedick now seems to be giving marriage — and women — the benefit of the doubt.

In general, women are seen as excuses for some good jokes and discussions to start with, but while Claudio puts Hero on a pedestal and worships her from a distance, Benedick really seems to want to make Beatrice happy — for her sake, not his ('they seem to pity the lady...' he says, as if he feels sympathy too for Beatrice).

Reasonable summing up but it introduces new point about power/control which hasn't really been explored earlier.

But in the end, Shakespeare still shows that men are the ones in control — because even if Benedick does change and show a softer side we must remember that it is the powerful Don Pedro who sets it all up.

Good contrast between different views about women from characters but what is Shakespeare saying about women here?

Marker's summary

- This is a very competent response which even tries to bring in social and cultural references about Shakespeare's times. There are many good points made with some useful supporting quotations.

- On occasions, the points are not developed enough and one or two points drift from the central task. It is no good saying what the characters' attitude to women is if this is not linked to what Shakespeare is saying.

- The student ends with an interesting point about control and power but this perhaps needed to be explored more fully to start with.

- This would gain a **low level 7**.

QUICK CHECK Section 1

Unit 1 Brush up your Shakespeare!

1. Timbreo (Claudio) and Fenicia (Hero)
2. Leonato's wife, Innogen
3. He played it every year for 30 years from 1748.
4. A ruler of Sicily – an illegitimate Prince of the House of Arragon (also named John).
5. They were masked balls with music, poetry, use of scenery and costumes, and were especially popular with the English Court between 1600 and 1640.
6. Romeo and Juliet

Unit 2 The plot

Act 1
1. Leonato's
2. Don Pedro, Benedick and company
3. Benedick
4. Hero
5. Benedick says that he will never marry.
6. The illegitimate half-brother of Don Pedro.
7. He overhears it while hiding behind a curtain (an 'arras').
8. Don John feels that Claudio has replaced him in his brother's affections and he therefore dislikes him.

Act 2
1. Masks
2. He says that Don Pedro secretly plans to marry her, himself.
3. Benedick and Beatrice
4. Borachio will fool Don Pedro and Claudio into thinking Hero is unfaithful. He will do this by getting Margaret to dress up in Hero's clothing, and appear at Hero's window with him.
5. They set up a conversation which they allow Benedick to overhear, in which they 'reveal' that Beatrice secretly loves him.
6. He begins to consider the benefits of marriage.
7. He believes there are secret messages of love in them.

Act 3
1. Hero sets up the actual deception, although it is Don Pedro who originally suggested they should do this.
2. Act 2 Scene 3
3. Pale, clean and newly-shaven (actually love-sick).
4. He will shame Hero at her own wedding by denouncing her, and rejecting her.
5. Dogberry and Verges
6. Conrade and Borachio
7. She seems 'distracted' and ill.
8. Love-sick (in love)
9. They are confusing and Leonato is in a hurry.
10. He is on his way to his daughter's wedding.

Act 4
1. Hero and Claudio
2. To take his daughter back (i.e. he refuses to marry her).
3. As a 'rotten orange'
4. Don Pedro and Don John
5. She faints.
6. Beatrice and the Friar (then Benedick)
7. They will pretend Hero is dead.
8. Conrade and Borachio
9. Dogberry's confusing language delays things, until the Sexton sorts it out.
10. He has fled/escaped from Messina.

Act 5
1. Leonato, Antonio (his brother) and Benedick
2. Claudio makes fun of Benedick. (He thinks Benedick is joking.)
3. He tells them Don John has fled from Messina.
4. They should proclaim Hero's innocence to the people of Messina, and Claudio must marry a niece of Leonato's he has never met (the next day).
5. All night
6. Her face is covered.
7. Secret love poems they have written are produced.
8. He kisses her.
9. A messenger
10. Don John has been captured and has been brought back to Messina.

Unit 3 The characters

Benedick
1. Away fighting alongside Don Pedro.
2. He says it is for fools – he will remain a bachelor.
3. He sees the benefits of marriage.
4. To kill Claudio.
5. Padua
6. He is 'loved' by them.
7. Beatrice
8. Benedick kisses her.

Beatrice
1. She refers to their 'last conflict' (a previous argument/battle).
2. Hero
3. Hero and Ursula
4. That he kill Claudio.
5. He says her beauty 'exceeds' (is greater than) Hero's.
6. She cannot bear the idea that people feel she cannot show love, so resolves to change.

Claudio
1. A messenger
2. Don John feels Claudio has replaced him in his brother's affections, and he is envious.
3. That Don Pedro wishes to marry her.
4. Benedick says Claudio is no longer the soldier he was, who once loved the drum and fife (used in battles).
5. He rejects her.
6. Claudio believes she has been unfaithful and is not 'pure'.
7. She condemns it and says evidence against Hero is very weak.
8. He should marry Leonato's other niece whom he has never seen, and pray at the family monument all night.

Hero
1. Leonato
2. Don Pedro
3. Ursula
4. Hero has no mother (at least none mentioned) and all his hopes are focused on her.
5. She faints.
6. The Friar, then Beatrice
7. Her face is covered.
8. She produces copies of love poems Beatrice has written.

Unit 4 Themes

Tricks and deception
1. A masked Don Pedro woos Hero for Claudio; Antonio tries to trick Ursula (unsuccessfully); Beatrice criticises and insults Benedick, who, though masked is recognised by her (not that she tells him).

2 They are both 'set up' to overhear conversations about themselves.

3 Margaret

4 Claudio appears as if he is about to go through with the marriage, so he can shame Hero publicly.

Self-deception

1 He believes all women love him; he also believes he is basically cold-hearted and has no romantic or emotional side; he is sure he will remain a bachelor.

2 He no longer uses joking language and says he despises their 'gossip-like humours'.

Love and marriage

1 Yes – he refers to when he first saw her (i.e. before this present meeting).

2 He is young (in appearance).

3 She speaks about Benedick: '...is Signor Mountanto returned from the wars yet?'

4 Yes – she refers to their 'last conflict'.

5 To stop her speaking, perhaps.

Status and honour

1 None

2 That's fine – providing she likes the husband he selects for her.

3 Beatrice (along with the Friar)

4 Because he arranged the marriage, and is therefore associated with a 'common stale' (a prostitute), as he refers to Hero.

Unit 5 Use of language

Lots of talk

1 They overhear others talking about them.

2 He is overheard revealing how Hero was made to look unfaithful.

3 Don John (he says so himself).

4 He is the one whose actions have the greatest impact – setting up the deception (which is a visual one).

5 Not in the end, though it does delay the truth.

6 A written poem.

7 The one between Claudio and Benedick; and the one between Leonato and Antonio, and Claudio and Don Pedro.

Puns and word play

1 'Nothing' may have been pronounced 'noting' which also means watching and observing.

2 They are saying they only fell for each other out of 'pity'.

3 'Mine' (about Hero)

Images and metaphors

1 Don John

2 As a 'witch'.

3 Hero, according to Claudio.

4 Borachio's

5 Beatrice refers to 'repentance' and of course Hero will live to regret her own first wedding.

Dogberry's use of language

1 Mixing words up, or inventing new ones unintentionally, which have the opposite meaning to that which is desired.

2 He misunderstands the word 'tedious' and says he will give lots of 'tediousness' to Leonato.

3 No one has recorded (written down) Conrade's insult.

4 No one can make sense of Dogberry's explanation.

QUICK CHECK Section 2

Unit 1 Understanding the question

Focus: Character and motivation
Key words: **What different impressions** do **we** get of **Leonato** in these **two scenes?**

Unit 2 Finding and using evidence

Possible answer: At the beginning of the scene the Friar is very much in his role and getting on with the job of marrying the two young people. When the trouble starts and Hero is shamed, he says nothing, choosing to retreat and 'stand back', presumably taking in what is around but not becoming 'hot-headed' or judgmental. We see this after Hero faints, presumed dead, and the Friar offers comfort to a distressed Beatrice, implying that Hero is at peace.

Angry Leonato contrasts greatly with the Friar here, which highlights the Friar's peaceful and gentle outlook. We see this in his response to Leonato's '*Dost thou look up?*' The Friar responds that he sees no reason why Hero should not be in heaven – unlike her own 'loving' father.

The Friar is a fair and calm man and sees the truth of Hero's nature largely through remaining 'an observer'. He invites Leonato, who is beside himself, to '*Hear me a little, for I have only been silent so long...*' He is able to show Leonato, and the audience, the benefits of not talking, as it is he who is able to see the truth of Hero's 'virtue' and '*the errors that these princes hold*'. It is owing to the Friar's advice that the truth is able to come out in the end, as he wisely advises Leonato to '*pause awhile*' and announce Hero's death. This allows time from some reflection away from all the over-reacting.

Unit 3 Paraphrasing, summarising and using quotations

Possible answer: It is clear that Claudio wants to point out how appearances can deceive, and that on the surface, when looking at Hero, most would '*...swear...she were a maid,*' that's to say, innocent and pure.

Unit 4 Structuring your answer

Possible adjectives:
Act 3 Scene 1 unsuspecting (1) resolved (3) shocked (2)
Act 5 Scene 4 proud (4) obedient (6) witty (5)

Unit 5 Writing about two scenes

The opening scene presents love as a game with formal rules and ways of acting, while the last scene presents characters who now face the reality of what love means, having been changed by what they have gone through.

In the first scene, Claudio asks Benedick's opinion of Hero. He asks '*Can the world buy such a jewel?*' showing his immature approach to love. Hero is merely a beautiful object, he does not know her and requires approval.

Unit 6 What makes a top answer

Suggested improvement: When Don Pedro is asked why he's not saying anything, it's clear he feels 'dishonoured' by his association with Hero, who he thinks is a 'common stale'. After all, he saw Hero being 'unfaithful' and, moreover, as the Prince, he can't afford to be made to look foolish, can he?